A

Down Memory Lane

A Stroll
Down Memory Lane

Growing-up in Post War Britain

Molly Brearley RGN, RM, RHV

Disclaimer

In the interest of privacy, certain names have been changed. Any resemblance to persons living or dead is purely coincidental.

Sister Kay was named Sister Brooks, and Miss Hickman was named Miss Hillman in my book *The Calling, Life as a Student Nurse in the 1960s.*

A CIP catalogue record for this book is available from the British Library.

ISBN 978-0-9954759-2-2

Book layout and cover design by Clare Brayshaw

Prepared and printed by:

York Publishing Services Ltd
64 Hallfield Road
Layerthorpe
York YO31 7ZQ

Tel: 01904 431213

Website: www. yps-publishing. co. uk

Molly holding the family dog Rex, sister Jane (middle) and cousin John (left)

Playing out with no time to pull their socks up!

Contents

CHAPTER 1

Earliest Memory

I must have been around four. I'm on the beach with Mum and Dad. Other members of the family are with us. I've just come out of the sea as I feel wet and cold in my elasticated swimsuit. It sticks to my skin as Mum slowly peels it off, and then dries me with a rough towel. The sun is shining brightly but there's a slight wind coming off the sea and I shiver as Mum quickly dresses me. The tide by now is far out. Seagulls can be heard squawking high in the sky. A small group of us run down to the shore. I imagine they are my cousins and older sister. We crouch in the shimmering sand, picking up seashells, water pooling round the dips made by the weight of our feet. The adults relax in deckchairs sheltering behind a windbreak. I suppose we are on our seaside holiday in Scarborough. I don't remember much about my life before this.

CHAPTER 2

Safely Delivered

I was born in Cullingworth on February 19, 1948, less than four years after the end of World War Two. It was a good place to be born.

Cullingworth is a village and civil parish in the City of Bradford, West Yorkshire. Historically part of the West Riding of Yorkshire, it is seven miles west of Bradford, three miles south of Keighley and several miles from the tourist magnet of Haworth, home of the Bronte sisters. It is nestled in Yorkshire's wonderful South Pennines. The surrounding countryside is mainly used for sheep and cattle farming with areas of moorland lying to the north-west. The village clings to a steep valley slope above Ellar Carr Beck with the dramatic hills, valleys and moorland providing an outstanding backdrop.

Like many West Yorkshire villages, Cullingworth was largely an agricultural settlement until the arrival of the textile industry in the 18th and 19th centuries. Powered first by water then by local coal, the boom in cloth production brought a huge increase in population and housing. The opening of the railway in 1884 further introduced the major features of Victorian life to a small Yorkshire hamlet. The inhabitants worked in the village mills, coal mining or quarrying the building stone from the millstone grit of the moors.

I was told that Mum had a long, painful labour. The front parlour was ready with a bed-settee in place for my arrival and the lying-in period. A roaring coal fire made the room feel cosy against the chilly February weather. Sister Wilson, the District Midwife, a small plump lady with tightly permed greying hair and a stern face, had visited that morning instructing my mother to keep busy as it would be a good while before the baby arrived. Believing she was only in early labour, Mum decided to do some cleaning upstairs to take her mind off her severe backache, but the pain became unbearable. Fortunately, Grandma Clark, my paternal grandmother, was in the house and realising that Mum was almost ready to push sent for the Midwife. Grandma was sitting with Mum on the stair steps when a flustered Sister Wilson arrived. Between them they managed to help her down the stairs and onto the bed with Sister Wilson protecting the top of my head with its black curly hair. I was safely delivered at 28 Mill Street before Dr Baird arrived. He was furious with Sister Wilson, giving her a good telling off before calmly checking that mother and child had no ill effects from their traumatic ordeal.

Helen, my half-sister, soon arrived home from school to find Mum comfortably tucked up in bed with Grandma sitting on a chair holding a baby wrapped in a cosy blanket. Helen hadn't a clue what was happening. She didn't know we were getting a baby. "Come over and have a look at your new baby sister," whispered Grandma. "We're going to call her Molly." It was such a surprise for Helen, who at the age of nine knew little about babies or where they came from. But she was so excited to have a baby sister she ran straight back to school to tell her teacher the good news.

Mum spent the following ten days in bed, with friends and family looking after her. It was such a busy household with a constant stream of people calling to see her and the new baby. Even the milkman would pop his head round the door each morning as he was delivering the milk. Mum was relieved when the lying-in-period was over.

CHAPTER 3

28 Mill Street

Our house was near the top in a long terrace of stone houses. The primary school was at the top and the village was at the bottom end. It was a small house with the front door leading right into the parlour, the "best room", which was only used for special occasions. Straight ahead was a dark lobby with hooks on the wall to hang coats and a space on the floor to store shoes. A steep staircase led from the lobby upstairs. Our kitchen and living room were at the back of the house. Mum was the mainstay of the family and always seemed to be busy preparing meals, baking, washing and ironing. The solid wood kitchen table would be covered in utensils and saucepans.

Upstairs were two bedrooms and a bathroom. I shared the back bedroom with Helen. It was a dark room with a small window overlooking the garden. We had a long garden set out in true post-war fashion: neat lawn, colourful flowerbeds, a vegetable patch at the top. In the distance we could see the local church spire, and we would hear the church bells chiming on the hour and half hour. At the top of the garden was the piggery. In the early days Dad used it for growing tomatoes and storing his garden equipment. The gate at the top of the garden opened onto a country lane, which led up to the primary school.

Mum and Dad had the front bedroom which overlooked the street. Although there were not many cars then it was noisier than our bedroom, with the early-morning milkman, delivery vans selling tea, fish and bread, plus the coalman and the occasional rag-and-bone man with his horse and cart collecting everything you put outside the front door. The Friendly Inn at the bottom of the street didn't help matters. The noise often went on until late at night when people could be heard shouting to each other as they staggered home.

Mum had three older siblings, two of whom, Auntie Linda and Uncle Clifford, lived in the village. Auntie Linda was a rotund lady with a pleasing smile and placid nature. She lived with Uncle Albert, a wiry man with short dark hair. He was like a whippet, always rushing around. Christopher was their eldest son. He was adopted as Auntie Linda had been told she'd never be able to have children. She was surprised when Cousin John arrived many years later! As a child I enjoyed visiting the family especially during the winter months when Auntie Linda would be sitting in front of the fire, dress hitched up exposing the elastic in her pink bloomers, her legs mottled from the heat of the flames. She'd frequently be tucking into a tin of biscuits swilled down with a pot of tea. She eventually developed type 2 diabetes.

Uncle Clifford was a smart, well-dressed man. He was softly spoken, hardworking, and devoted to his family. He lived with Auntie Nora and their three young daughters, Janet, Jean and Joyce.

The eldest of Mum's siblings, Auntie Ada, lived in Haworth. She was always immaculately dressed in brightly coloured clothes and rarely seen without her lipstick. In later life following a fall, the ambulance men had to wait for her to put her "lippy" on before taking her to hospital. She lived in a large terraced house with Uncle Gilbert and children James, Brian and Marlene.

Grandma and Grandad Field, my maternal grandparents, lived nearby. I can't remember much about Grandad as he died when I was young but Grandma played a major role in my upbringing. She was such a character and joy to be with but didn't stand for any nonsense.

Grandma Clark had moved to the village from Scotland following the death of her husband, the year before my birth. Dad was her only living child. Her son Louie had died in childhood and her daughter Bessie had died as a young woman. Grandma Clark was a large, solemn lady who rarely smiled. She didn't do fun things like Grandma Field but she was a good baker. When I visited her on baking day, she would be red-faced and covered in flour. I always left with a bag full of goodies.

CHAPTER 4

Peacetime

Dad was born in Canada, but while still an infant his Scottish parents returned to their home near Motherwell, where he was brought up. He married his first wife Isabella in 1937 and Helen was born the following year. Isabella sadly died two months after the birth from anaemia and cardiac failure. She was only 24 years old. Dad, standing at her graveside holding their baby in his arms, must have been a pitiful sight. Several months later his sister Bessie died age 27 of tuberculosis of lung and abdomen. Dad had no time to grieve as later that year he joined the forces as war broke out. His parents took care of Helen. Dad met Mum at a dance when he was stationed in Yorkshire. Dad was ten years her senior and was very handsome and mature. They married at the parish church in Cullingworth on June 27, 1942.

Mum was born in Castleford before her family moved to Cullingworth. She had loving parents and a happy childhood. She had worked in the local mill since leaving school and had a good circle of friends. Mum had never been away from home, so it was a difficult time for the family when she moved to Scotland to live with Dad's parents and learn how to care for Helen during the war years. Unhappy times were to follow. Mum was only 15 years older than Helen and had no experience of young children. Although Grandma remained firmly in charge, Mum found it overwhelming and she desperately missed her family and friends back in Yorkshire.

The year of my birth found Mum, Dad and Helen settled in our new family home in Cullingworth. It must have been a difficult time of adjustment, with the war over and Dad out of the army working hard trying to make a living, Mum becoming a housewife and Helen leaving all her friends back in Scotland and starting a new school. Times were hard for most families back then.

I wasn't an easy child by all accounts. I cried a lot and refused to sleep as a young baby, only settling when rocked to sleep. I developed well and started talking at an early age, but my behaviour continued to be very trying at times. Helen dreaded having to take me shopping with her. While she was getting served, I would stand looking up at the large wooden counter asking, "What does Molly want?" If she guessed incorrectly, the question would be repeated, and so it continued until a long queue of customers formed behind us, impatiently waiting to be served. Once she guessed what I wanted she quickly paid the bill and rushed me out of the shop clutching my bag of sweets. Fortunately, my behaviour improved and I grew into a sociable, happy little girl.

Mum was a pretty young lady, petite with short dark brown hair and a clear complexion. She was always smartly dressed and loved to wear her high-heeled shoes. Mum was happy being a housewife in her new home, though life then for the average married woman was very different from how it is today. Very few women worked after getting married. They stayed at home to keep house and raise the children.

It was still unusual for women to go into further education, especially working-class women. Girls were prepared for this life, learning from their mothers and with lessons at senior school on cooking, household management, sewing and ironing.

Dad was a dashing young man with jet-black hair and brown eyes. He was very much the head of the household, dealing with the money and paying the bills. Only the family allowance was paid directly to my mother, but Dad would sort his wage out so she never went short.

My parents struggled to make ends meet and Dad often did extra work cleaning windows and chimney sweeping in his free time. But we were no better off and no worse off than anyone else we knew. We were the working class. The after-effects of the war were ongoing, many goods still being rationed in the early 1950s. Sugar was rationed until 1953 and meat only came off ration a year later. I don't remember food rationing as we were always well fed as children, Dad's vegetable garden coming to the rescue when needed.

CHAPTER 5

Childhood Days

In the 1950s the camaraderie of wartime was still evident throughout the country. Families stayed together through the hard times and everybody knew their neighbours and had a sense of belonging. It was a happy time for little children like me to be growing up. The environment then felt much safer than today, and children were allowed the freedom of being outside from an early age, playing rough-and-tumble games, climbing and getting dirty, often covered in cuts and bruises. There were no pre-schools or nurseries, so we didn't start school until we almost turned five. The 'Bobby on the Beat' got to know the neighbourhood and the characters who lived there and people felt it was safe to walk the streets. There was little vandalism and no graffiti. Telephone boxes were fully glazed and each contained a set of local telephone directories and a pay box full of pennies. Youngsters respected and feared people in authority, knowing that they would get a clip around the ear if caught misbehaving.

I liked spending time at home, mostly in the kitchen or out in the garden. I enjoyed putting my apron on, rolling my sleeves up and washing my hands for inspection ready to help with the baking. I would drag the stool-steps over to the kitchen table, pull the steps down and climb up. Mum would give me the leftover bits of pastry to play with. I loved rolling it out with my rolling pin and making something for Dad when he came home from work. He was always delighted, but I doubt he ever tasted any of it. My favourite job was helping to make a cake. There was always some sponge mixture left in the bowl for me to eat; the bowl was easily washed when I'd finished with it! I was so excited when the cake was ready and couldn't wait for it to cool before sampling it.

Mum was always busy. Housework in those days was a full-time job. It was very labour-intensive without today's gadgets and there were no such things as convenience foods or fast-food outlets. Sweets and crisps were treats rather than everyday foods. Mum took pleasure and pride in looking after her home and family to the best of her ability.

Monday was washday in most households. It wasn't just popping clothes into the machine and then into the tumble dryer. Mum would either wash by hand using a rubbing board or use the electric washing machine with its mangle. The machine would noisily wash the clothes, then Mum would hook them out with large wooden tongs and put them through the mangle. I liked to watch her put the wet clothes between the two large rollers, turning the wheel with the hand crank as the water was wrung out. Washing was a laborious job leaving the kitchen dull, steamy and damp.

My mother saved hard to buy a twin-tub washing machine. It must have been a godsend at that time but proved to be a bit of a palaver as the machine was not plumbed in. It came with two hoses, one for filling the tub and the other for emptying the other tub. As neither the filling nor the emptying was automatic and time had to be spent passing clothes from one tub to the other, someone had to stand over the machine a lot of the time. After the rinsing was finally completed the clothes were hooked out often wound together. As Mum unravelled the clothes she would shake her head saying, "I would have had the washing on the line by now with my old machine."

On a fine day all the neighbours would be hanging out their washing and chatting to each other. All the washing lines would be full by lunchtime, clothes secured by large wooden pegs. On one side of us were Rhoda and Billy Atkinson. Rhoda was a small, plump lady with greying ginger hair and a pale complexion. She was very house-proud, and liked her whites to be the whitest in the street. The couple went on holiday to Morecambe each year. Rhoda would return with a bright-red face and dry, peeling skin, proving they'd had good weather. The elderly neighbours on the other side were Mr and Mrs Peacock. They were a delightful couple, often inviting me over to have a chat if I was playing in the garden. Mrs Peacock never mentioned her whites!

Now I was passed the "What does Molly want?" stage, shopkeepers and customers were happy to see me. Shopping was done every day as storing fresh food was difficult. There were no supermarkets so we had to visit many shops and carry everything home in a basket. I felt very grown-up carrying my own wicker basket. As we were on a tight budget, Mum would have to be careful what she spent. My favourite shop was the fruit shop in Francis Square. It was a small shop packed full of brightly coloured fruit and vegetables well displayed and hard to resist. Connie and Harry Gibbons owned the shop and lived there with their daughter Marilynne. Connie was a very attractive lady who had lived in the village most of her life and knew everybody, so it wasn't surprising when the queue extended outside of the shop. But nobody minded as Connie and Harry had the time to spend with each customer. The next shop was The Co-op where Mum bought things like bread, butter, cheese, tinned fruit, evaporated milk and Heinz salad cream. Then on the way home we'd call at Passman's Butchers at the bottom of Mill Street for mince, sausages or pork chops.

Some foods had to be purchased and cooked straight away as we couldn't store them. We only had a freestanding kitchen larder cupboard for storage. It was pale green with two cupboards at the bottom, glass cupboards at the top and a pull-down cupboard in the middle providing a work top. Meat and fish were stored on a cold tin plate until cooked and milk was placed in a bucket of cold water.

We didn't have fitted carpets in those days. The floors were covered with large carpet squares and rugs laid on polished linoleum. Mum cleaned the carpets with a carpet sweeper before the vacuum cleaner arrived. I helped to polish the linoleum by skating round the room in my socks. The carpets and rugs were often taken outside and hung on the clothes line. Then Mum would beat them with a carpet beater to get rid of the muck from the coal fires. It must have worked wonders for her upper body strength but covered her in clouds of dust. A wooden clothes prop was used to raise the line and enable the rugs to catch the breeze.

The vague memories of my pre-school days are happy ones. I didn't see many children my own age but learnt to socialise with older children and adults. I enjoyed playing alone and never felt lonely as my imaginary friends were always around. On the day I started school Mum rushed around making sure I was fed and smartly dressed before we stepped out into the busy street.

Molly

Me with Dad

Me aged 3 years with Mum

Playing in the street

Visiting Mrs Peacock next door

Smiling for the camera

Amusing Mrs Peacock's grandchild

CHAPTER 6

Starting School

Cullingworth Village Primary School was a Victorian building originally opened in 1881. It was small, with only five classrooms, but was at the heart of village life with strong community links.

My first day at school was a shock to the system. It was the first time I had been on my own away from home and apart from Mum. It was a very tearful event for the children and very upsetting for the parents. We arrived to find a queue of neatly turned-out children clinging to their mums at the school door. We were the 'Baby Boomers' named after the explosion of babies born following the end of the Second World War. The number of babies born during this time was roughly 50 per cent higher than average, so class sizes when I started school were large.

School photograph

Mrs Boothman was our teacher, a slim lady with a solemn face and dark, greying hair neatly pinned back. She was well dressed in dark skirt and jacket, white blouse and laced-up shoes. As there were no classroom assistants, she was in for a stressful day organising her new intake of around 30 unhappy children. We spent the day playing and getting used to the school environment. I felt lost, as it was my first interaction with a group of other children, but at least Marilynne from the fruit shop was in my class. The next day I couldn't understand why I had to go to school again as I thought I'd already been! I was surprised to learn that school continued for many years.

Having got over the pangs of separation, school life soon fell into a predictable routine. It started at 9am and finished at 4pm as a rule. Not many parents would drive their children to school, mainly because not many people had cars. There was no such thing as health and safety or children's rights. You were taught discipline at home and at school. Teachers were very strict in those days and allowed to use corporal punishment to enforce discipline. We had to be on our best behaviour in Mrs Boothman's class or we got smacked. I was shocked as my parents were strict but they had never smacked me. Learning was not constructed with the National Curriculum; there were no detailed reports and no Ofsted inspections. Instead there were school inspectors who paid visits to see what was going on.

Formal education started early in school. It was very much a 'talk and chalk' approach with the teacher standing at the front of the class and the children sitting at desks facing the blackboard. Reading, Writing and Arithmetic (the three 'R's) were very important. A lot of learning was done by rote and chanting times tables seemed to be a daily thing. It must have worked as I've never forgotten them. I enjoyed learning to read and write. Neat handwriting and correct spelling were seen to be very important. We would often go on nature walks, learning about the countryside and collecting things such as leaves to bring back to school to study.

The School Broadcasting Council for the United Kingdom had been set up in 1947 and the wireless or radio played a large part in the education of school children. I enjoyed music and movement where we would jump and run around to the instructions on the radio. As we didn't have a gym kit in primary school we removed our outer clothes and exercised in vests, knickers or underpants and either pumps or bare feet. Physical education was often done outside unless it was very cold, wet or snowy.

School milk was part of the routine, detested by most of the children. In post-war Britain school milk, a third of a pint per day, was introduced to supplement the child's diet. In 1971 school milk for the over-sevens was withdrawn by Margaret Thatcher, then Secretary of State for Education. For this she was dubbed "Thatcher, Thatcher, milk snatcher" in the press. It was fascinating to see the small crates of milk outside the school on a cold winter's morning with the shiny bottle tops standing proud above the columns of frozen milk. The milk was defrosted by the radiator before we reluctantly drank the watery, lukewarm liquid.

School dinners were made on site, the aroma of vegetables and warm custard filling the school. Dinners were basic, simple and filling – meat and two veg, fish on Fridays, cooked dessert such as rice pudding, semolina, tapioca jam sponge and custard. Mum would send me to school with my dinner money each week but the very poor children got free meals. We had a rest after dinner while we were in Mrs Boothman's class. Mats were placed on the floor in the hall and we had to lay quietly with eyes closed. Some children managed to fall asleep while others were bored and fidgety.

Regular visits from the school nurse would break up the school routine. The nit nurse often referred to as "Nitty Nora" would check all the children for head lice. Each class would march into the hall and line up to be examined in turn, their hair closely scrutinised for any signs of infestation. Routine hearing and vision tests were also done by the school nurse. Children had a medical check by the school doctor when they started school and again before they left.

We all dreaded the visit by the school dentist who used to come around every so often and look in our mouths. Dreadful stories were put about by the other children as to how bad the experience was going to be and I became frightened about the forthcoming ordeal. There was a lack of knowledge around dental health at the time and a lot of children had not visited the dentist before. I clearly remember our family dentist. His name was Mr Spoor, a lanky, pale-faced man with floppy fair hair and gold teeth. Mum had found him when she was suffering from severe toothache. She had caught the bus to Keighley and traipsed around the town in search of a dentist. Mr Spoor was the only one who agreed to treat her that day. So for years I was taken to this eccentric dentist who walked about with a silver-grey Siamese cat on his shoulder. The surgery was in a large terrace house. I recall the faint smell of anaesthetic on entering the dark hallway before turning right into the waiting room. People would be sitting anxiously waiting their turn; the only sound was the clock ticking or the odd cough. I would sit stock-still waiting for the dental nurse to come and march me upstairs to the treatment room. It was an awful experience as Mum wasn't allowed to stay with me. I clearly remember the day I had two milk teeth removed. Mr Spoor was waiting dressed in his white coat and mask. The nurse helped me onto a black chair facing the window. I could see a tray full of shiny instruments and a large drill operated by a series of pulleys from the corner of my eye. Mr Spoor was talking incessantly to the nurse as he washed his hands and put his gloves on. No explanation was given as I was held down and a large mask put on my face. I dreamt of elephants before waking up to the sun streaming through the window and blood pouring out of my mouth. We visited Mr Spoor for many years. Mum argued he was a good dentist. She was probably right as he gave plenty of anaesthetic before filling teeth; your mouth remained numb for two days but the filling lasted for many years.

I'd made lots of friends and gained confidence at school before going into the second year. As we lived nearby, I could listen for the bell to ring before running up the lane. The Headmaster, Mr Baker, would often be standing proudly in the doorway to greet his pupils. I felt so grown-up hanging my coat on the peg, going into the class and sitting at my desk. I was never late for lessons. I was in Miss Chapman's class for the next two years. She was a pretty young lady with short reddish hair and a gentle manner. She didn't smack us like Mrs Boothman. She was a good teacher who made lessons interesting. Miss Chapman was very particular about cleanliness and would often check our hands and nails were clean. We didn't wear school uniform in junior school, but most children were clean and well dressed. Some of the poorer children who were smelly and unkempt were often laughed at and picked on by the other children.

One day I started to feel poorly at school. I felt tired, had a runny nose, red watery eyes and didn't eat much dinner. Mum thought I had a cold but a few days later when I developed an itchy rash around my head and neck I was kept off school. When the rash started to spread over my body she sent for Dr Baird who soon arrived with his black case to check me over. I had measles which, like German measles and mumps, was a common childhood illness in the 1950s. I had to stay in bed and drink plenty of water. My eyes were very sore and Mum cleaned them with damp cotton wool, closed the curtains and covered the light to protect my eyesight. Dr Baird visited daily until I recovered; my mother always said he was "a good attender". I was busy writing on my blackboard when he last visited. He was so impressed with my neat handwriting that I didn't wipe it off for weeks.

Measles vaccine was developed in 1963, with an improved version becoming widely available in 1968. The NHS began vaccinating for measles in 1968 as soon as this second, safer vaccine was available. Vaccines were also available to protect against mumps and rubella in the late 1960s. These three vaccines were combined into the MMR vaccine in 1971.

Dr Baird had been Mum's family doctor for many years and was well respected in the village. He held his surgery in rented rooms in a large detached house on Station Road. No appointment was necessary; you just sat in the front lounge and waited your turn. If you were ill on Saturday morning, a surgery was held in the back room of Bert Dawson's cobbler's shop. Customers would come into the shop with shoes for repair, while patients sat discussing their ailments, waiting to see the doctor. It was like a social gathering.

Miss Goodyear was my teacher in year four, a small, scary-looking lady who stood no nonsense from her pupils. The work was much harder and we had to sit quietly and pay attention at all times. She was in full command and there was rarely the need for punishment. We had a weekly spelling test. Words were copied from the blackboard and taken home to learn before the following day's test. She expected full marks. Miss Goodyear was an excellent teacher and I learnt so much in her class.

Miss Johns taught us the following year. She was a posh, blonde-haired lady who kept bees. One day we arrived in class to find a large centrifuge extractor plus honeycombs in the middle of the floor. It was hard to imagine how it had all got there. Miss Johns, eager to show us how honey was made, selected a few of her favourite pupils to help her. They could take it in turns to wind the handle of the machine while we observed the honey being extracted from the honeycombs. All was going well until it was Andrea's turn and she accidently dropped a penny into the honey. Miss Johns was so angry the honey had been contaminated. Red faced she glared at her before shouting, "Andrea, if it hadn't been you I would have given you a slap." Andrea wasn't punished because she was a bright girl from a very wealthy family. I never liked Miss Johns and can only remember learning about bees in her class.

By the time I reached the upper class, Mr Baker had left the school and Mr Bell was now the Headmaster. He was a large man with a big voice and an authoritative manner. Mr Bell taught most of our lessons and never missed a thing. I sat near the back and recall the last lesson one Friday when we had to do some quiet reading. Mr Bell was sitting at his desk busy working so I decided to have a rest. I was relieved when his loud voice instructed us to close our books as I was keen to go home. He stood and, looking around the class, said in a loud voice, "Could Molly please stand up and tell us what she has been reading about?" I went bright red as I confessed I hadn't read anything.

Back then there was no comprehensive system. It was the age of the 11-plus, a series of tests and exams we had to take in the top class at primary school. Introduced in 1944, the examination was used to determine whether you went into secondary or grammar school education. We had an English and Maths paper plus puzzles and problem-solving questions to complete. My Cousin Janet was training to be a teacher at the time and had to find someone to complete the exam for her to mark. I was the obvious victim and passed the exam with no problem. Unfortunately, I failed the 11-plus examination at school, so would be going to Bingley Secondary Modern School with most of the other children. Only a few were offered a place at grammar school.

The baby boomer generation was particularly affected because grammar school places had not been sufficiently increased to accommodate the large rise in student numbers entering secondary education. As a result, cut-off standards on the 11-plus examination for entry into grammar school rose and many students who would, in earlier years, have been streamed into grammar schools were sent to secondary moderns. I often wonder how many children passed the exam but were denied a grammar school education due to lack of spaces. The education system at that time must have failed many children.

School leaving photo – Aged 11 years

I am second from the right (bottom row), my friend Marilynne Gibbons is 3rd from the right (bottom row), friend Andrea Kemp is on the left (middle row) friend Susan Ingham 3rd from left (top row) with Mr Bell (Headmaster) on the left

CHAPTER 7

A New Arrival

I was six when my sister Jane was born and don't remember any particular discussion about it during the pregnancy. It was all kept hush-hush. I knew there was something secretive going on: Mum kept being sick and Auntie Linda and Grandma Field were always around helping her in the house while whispering to each other. Was Mum poorly? I hadn't seen Dr Baird visiting but he might have been while I was at school. As a nosey child I became very curious and tried listening to the adult conversations whenever I could. I would creep downstairs at night when I should have been in bed and quietly sit on the stair step in the hope that Dad's loud voice would give me some clues. I never got caught. Mum soon stopped being sick and started wearing baggy clothes that looked too big for her. She then went away to get a new baby. I'd seen a crib in my parents' bedroom but hadn't been told we were getting a baby to put in it!

This was a time when childbirth and breastfeeding were not widely discussed. There was a lack of education around birth and some women were frightened about labour, not understanding what was happening. Years later, I remember Grandma Clark telling me she didn't even know how her first baby was going to come out, she just assumed it would pop out through her tummy button. What a shock it must have been to learn it was going to come out the same way it had gone in. It was all so different to today when pregnant ladies are proud to show off their pregnant bodies and are more knowledgeable about breastfeeding and childbirth.

It was still the norm for babies to be born at home, but my arrival had been such a fiasco that Mum decided to have a proper rest this time and went to St John's Hospital in Keighley to give birth. I have a clear memory of visiting her with Dad. The hospital looked so big from the eyes of a six-year-old. Tightly holding my father's hand we walked down a long corridor leading to Mum's ward where I was overwhelmed at the sight of all the beds and cots lined up neatly down each side. The new mothers were happily chatting while the nurses were busy rushing around making sure everything was shipshape. I couldn't take my eyes off the nurses, they looked so pretty in their long dresses with white aprons and white hats perched on top of their heads. Mum was sitting up in bed waiting for us. Smiling at me she said, "Come and have a look at your new baby sister before the nurse takes her back to the nursery." Feeling very proud to be a big sister, I tip-toed to the cot and peeped in to see a mop of blonde curly hair framing a little round face with chubby cheeks. Her big blue eyes were peeping over the blankets at me. I couldn't wait for her to come home. The babies had all been fed and were ready to go back to the nursery so we were soon ushered out so the mums could have a rest.

I was glad when my mother came home; she seemed to have been away for such a long time. Everything was ready for her arrival; no bed in the front room this time. Mum was relaxed and managing to feed Jane. Breastfeeding was a very private matter back then, and feeding in public places was a no-no. If we had visitors, Mum would be banished to another room to breastfeed as men and young children shouldn't witness the process. The word breast didn't seem to be used at all. Mum was often asked if she was feeding the baby herself and advised to drink stout as it would "help your milk". It was all very confusing for a six-year-old. Mum tried the stout but didn't like it. One day I sneaked into her bedroom when she was feeding. What was baby Jane doing chomping at Mum's chest? Was she eating her? That must be how you feed a baby yourself. I didn't ask and no explanation was given.

CHAPTER 8

Sugar and Spice

With the arrival of Jane and the nappies came the endless routine of feeding and changing. Mum's life was busier than ever now and she was always rushing around trying to get on top of things. Washday Monday suddenly became washday every day. The Terry towelling nappies used in those days were very different to today's disposables and it wasn't easy putting them on the baby. Firstly, the square nappy had to be folded crossways to make a triangle; it could be folded in half again making it a smaller triangle for a smaller baby. The baby was laid on the triangle with the long edge under the tummy and other edge between her legs. The three mini triangles poking out were then wrapped round the baby to overlap each other. Once mum had wrestled Jane into her nappy she had to securely pin it together with a large safety pin, making sure not to stab herself or the baby. If you could pick up your child without the nappy falling down it was a job well done. Cleaning the nappies was a laborious job. Any poo had to be scraped into the toilet before the nappies were placed in a metal bucket filled with water. I vaguely remember Mum then transferring them to a pan to be boiled and then thoroughly rinsed. Often, coming home from school, I would have to negotiate my way round a line full of white nappies before reaching the back door. In cold weather they would be frozen and brought into the house stiff like boards. In winter the house would be cluttered with clothes. We had a useful contraption in the kitchen called a ceiling airer which consisted of rigid horizontal wooden 'lines' which could be hauled up to the ceiling out of the way. As babies were changed around six times daily, it's no wonder they were potty trained much earlier than today.

Mum didn't get the chance to go out much but looked forward to pushing the pram to the village shops. There was no carting off kids to playgroups or soft play areas. Cars were a luxury and not many families could afford them. In 1950 there were less than two million cars in Great Britain with only 14 per cent of households owning one. The most popular models at this time included the Austin A35 Saloon and the Ford Prefect 100E. There were no child seats as we know them today. Baby would be put in a carrycot and placed on the back seat of the car, possibly wedged in. There were no seatbelts in the back until decades later. If we went to Keighley we would travel by bus or train. I enjoyed the excitement of the train ride. Helen remembers the journey with me as a baby. I had a big old pram with a wonky wheel and a brake that didn't work. As the pram was too big to fit on the train we had to travel in the guard's van. Unfortunately, the railway station in Cullingworth was closed to passengers in May 1955 apart from the odd excursion to Morecambe, Southport or the East Coast up to 1958. The track was finally lifted away in 1966.

My life didn't change much with the arrival of Jane as I continued to enjoy a happy carefree time. Grandma Field would sometimes pick me up from school and take me to her house for tea. It was a real treat as we always stopped at the sweet shop and left with a bag of sweets or crisps. Choosing sweets took ages as there were so many, but there was only one type of crisp. I liked to search for the little blue bag of salt in my packet of Smith's crisps, twist it open and sprinkle the salt on my crisps. If it was a nice day we would stop off at the War Memorial in the village, sit on one of the benches chatting and watching the world go by. I think Grandma was glad of the company since Grandad Field had died earlier that year and she now lived alone in her bungalow in Southfield Road. Grandma was a stoic Yorkshire woman, a round lady with a warm smile and clear complexion who was rarely seen without a scarf covering her short grey hair. She suffered from arthritis and one of her toe joints was so badly deformed she had to cut a hole in the top of her shoe to make room for it. I enjoyed helping Grandma clean her large collection of brasses, a job she did every two weeks. I collected the brasses, put them on newspaper and opened the tin of Brasso polish wadding. I didn't like the smell but got on with the polishing. By the end of the job the brasses were sparkling but my hands were black.

As a young child I didn't venture far from home. Auntie Linda lived in Lodge Street which ran parallel to Mill Street separated by a row of back-to-back houses and the YMCA building at the bottom of the streets. When visiting I often took the short cut through the ginnel between the Friendly pub and the YMCA.

John O'Connor was often seen in the ginnel making his way to the pub or staggering back from it. He was an elderly man who lived with his long-suffering wife in Lodge Street. She often found him slumped in the ginnel late at night when he had failed to make it home. He once unexpectedly visited our house when I was a young girl. "Is your little lass in?" he asked Mum as she opened the door. As I joined them he handed over a large bag full of sweets saying, "I've bought her some sweets cos she's the only little bugger that'll speak to me." He then turned on his heels and left. Years later when he died his wife looked soulless as she did her shopping. She missed having Johnny around. It took her a long while to get over his death.

Auntie Linda's door was always open; in the summer months it was often left wide open. She said they'd "nowt to pinch". I often sat for a while in the empty house and if they didn't appear would just leave. It was a cold, wet day near the end of the school holiday and none of my friends were playing out so I decided to pay her a visit. The house was empty apart from a chicken soaking in a sink full of water ready to be cooked. I knew she wasn't far away as potatoes and vegetables had been prepared ready for tea. I sat in the drab sitting room in front of the coal fire. I didn't wait long before the door flew open and in rushed a wet Uncle Albert. "Na then wasta doin ere lass? What yer bin up to?" he asked, surprised to see me.

"Nothing much. My friends aren't playing out so came to see if Auntie Linda was in," I replied.

"Nay, she's traipsing around shops wi John." Glancing at his wristwatch he continued: "They should be back any minute. It's nithering out theer today; bet your friends are all inside keeping warm. I'm putting kettle on, do you want summat to drink? We've got some pop if you'd like some." Uncle Albert soon joined me with his pint mug full of very strong tea and a glass of pop. "Help thissen to a biscuit lass," he said, pointing to the tin of biscuits sitting in pride of place on the table.

Auntie Linda soon waddled in with John in his pushchair. He must have been around two years old and looked far too big to be in a pushchair. Auntie Linda never imagined she'd have a child of her own. Did she want to keep him a baby for as long as possible?

"Hello Molly," she said, "how lovely to see you. I'll join you in a minute when I've sorted our John out." After removing her wet coat she was soon in her usual seat, still wearing her pinny and headscarf, tucking into the biscuits while Uncle Albert made her a cup of tea.

John was soon running around. He was as energetic as his father, a happy young boy with blond curly hair, a cheeky face and a wide smile exposing the largest dimples I'd ever seen. We had a long chat before it was time to leave.

"I'd better go home or Mum will be wondering where I am," I said, standing up ready to leave. "Okay, love. Tell your mum I'll pop up to see her tomorrow if she's in." As I walked through the kitchen Uncle Albert was lifting the chicken out of the sink and glancing out of the window. "It's teemin dahn again," he said, drying his hands and giving me a penny. "Get thissen some spice lass, tarra for now." The word 'spice' was a term used for sweets in West Yorkshire, generally by the older generation. I remember singing the "sugar and spice and all things nice" nursery rhyme as a young girl and gather sweets were originally made from sugar and spice or herbs, like cinnamon, mint and lavender.

Cousin Christopher, John's older adopted brother, was around the same age as Helen so we didn't have much in common. But I liked spending time with Chris and looked up to him as an older brother. He was quiet, intelligent and so good-looking. From a young age he had felt different from other boys and became very withdrawn, not wanting to be out with his friends. He spent lots of time indoors and Auntie Linda became very worried about him. Chris was gay, a homosexual to use the terminology of the day. It was misunderstood and not spoken about at that time.

It's difficult to imagine that, until the passing of the Sexual Offences Bill in 1967, male homosexual activity was illegal and was subject to public disapproval. For most people the sixties were a time of sexual awakening and experimentation. But it wasn't until 1967 that gay and bisexual men could share that freedom. On July 5, 1967, a bill to legalise homosexuality came through its final stages in the House of Commons. The Act was terribly flawed and didn't come close to equalising the legal status of homosexuals and heterosexuals, which would take many years. The single thing that more than any other has normalised gay relationships has been civil partnerships.

CHAPTER 9

The Great Storm

On Monday, June 11, 1956, around 6pm a violent thunderstorm broke over the Cullingworth area. It was no ordinary summer storm as it increased with such intensity that six-and-a-half inches of rain fell in the hour up to 7pm.

It had been a very humid day with other areas of the country reporting heavy downpours with thunder during the day. By teatime it had become unusually oppressive and gloomy and then raindrops as big as pan lids began to fall. We were all at home with Dad anxiously looking out of the kitchen window as the garden rapidly filled with water. He quickly banked up the back door afraid it would flood into the house. Helen and I were in our bedroom, me sitting on the windowsill and Helen standing beside me watching the storm. The rain became so heavy it could be heard on the roof. Unfortunately, our roof often leaked if there was a downpour and water soon started to drip through the bedroom ceiling. We hurried to put buckets and sheets on the carpet to keep it dry. And then the storm became a full-blown cloudburst with hail, fork lightning and thunderclaps every ten seconds. But throughout there was no wind; it remained very calm. However, the electricity failed, manhole covers blew and many houses were flooded. As the deluge stopped, the sun came out and the rest of the evening was fine and dry.

We were lucky as our house didn't flood. The worst effects were felt in the centre of the village. Although I was only eight years old at the time, I remember the sight of Halifax Road soon after the storm. It had suddenly become a river and people were standing outside their front doors or looking out of upstairs windows in disbelief. Walls were flattened, gardens and allotments ruined, huts washed away and poultry drowned. The road was covered with rocks and stones and buses struggled to get through. Bingley Urban District Council provided bottles of 1001 carpet cleaner for families with near-ruined carpets, but some houses were not habitable for many months.

Helen was 17 years old by this time and had grown into a very attractive young lady. She was petite with fragile facial features and porcelain skin. Her red hair was thick and wavy. Helen had left school at the age of 15 and worked in the local textile industry, burling and mending. This is the final stage of the worsted manufacturing process. It must have taken a lot of concentration as the finished cloth had to be inspected by sight and feel for imperfections and knots. These were then teased out and invisibly mended to leave a perfect length of fabric. It was a highly skilled job. Many women took in pieces of cloth to burl and mend at home. It was convenient if they had a young family.

The 1950s was a time when fashion exploded after the austerity of the war years with exciting new silhouettes, colours and prints. An hourglass figure dominated the look with cinched-in waistlines and accentuated hips and busts. Fashion trends included swing dresses with petticoats for fullness, slim-fitting dresses, tailored suits, Capri pants and pencil or circular skirts. Dresses and skirts were worn well below the knee. Money and materials were still in short supply. But part of feeling normal for many British women was in looking fashionable.

It wasn't until this decade that the age between child and adult was acknowledged. Teenagers began to break away from their mothers' stiff styling and develop their own look. There wasn't much for teenagers to do in our village, but Helen always looked nice when going to meet friends or going to the cinema. And I loved to watch her getting ready. It took ages and seemed such a palaver having so many clothes to put on. If she was wearing a gathered skirt or dress it all started with the pointiest bra, big knickers and a big girdle that had suspenders attached. Next came the petticoat, with several layers of net starched to make it extra stiff. Some petticoats showed below the skirt hem, trimmed in pretty colours. Helen sometimes wore a tight sweater or a cardigan backwards so the buttons were not visible from the front. A wide elastic belt, stockings and flat ballet shoes, and she was dressed at last. The look was completed with a pretty scarf in her hair and pop-it beads round her neck and wrist. The beads were one of the most ubiquitous fads at the time. Made of plastic, each bead connected to the next bead by a knob that made a popping sound when pushed in. They could be arranged into single or multi-strand bracelets and necklaces then taken apart to make different styles and colours. I would spend hours playing with them.

Helen left home soon after this and lived with Grandma Clark until she married at the age of 18.

CHAPTER 10

Playtime

A sense of belonging spilled out onto our street where I spent many happy hours with my new-found friends from primary school. We would meet in the school holidays and play out for hours, only popping home when we were hungry or needed a plaster for a grazed leg. Boys and girls played some street games together, but my favourite was hopscotch which was popular with the girls. We were allowed to chalk the board out on the pavement but had to clean up when we'd finished or we got into bother. Hours were spent playing ball, and skipping, marbles and jacks were also popular games. The street was a hive of activity by day and there was always someone around to keep an eye on us. Our front room looked out onto the pavement and in those days women prided themselves on having a well-scrubbed step and clean pavement outside their houses. It was a common sight on a dry day to see a row of women kneeling on mats busy scrubbing their steps while having a good gossip. I never knew why Mum scrubbed the step then painted a white line on the edge, but it probably made it more visible and prevented stumbling up or down it.

During the 1950s very few people had TV and it was very much second fiddle to the radio, often referred to as the wireless. Programmes, as during the war, steered towards being jolly and leaving your troubles behind you. The radio was popular with housewives and could often be heard out in the street. Morning radio was heavily slanted towards wives and mothers, career women being almost unheard of. Mum listened to *Housewives' Choice*, *Music While You Work* and *Mrs Dale's Diary*. In the afternoon there was usually a lunchtime drama which my mother would listen to if she got time to put her feet up before I came home from school. It is hard to believe there were no personal music players and the only music available was from the radio. It was the decade of skiffle with artists such as Lonnie Donegan. Rock and roll came in from the States with Bill Haley, Cliff Richard and the Shadows, and Elvis Presley. British singers became popular too, such as Marty Wilde, Billy Fury, Adam Faith and Tommy Steele. But the only way to hear modern popular music was to tune into Radio Luxembourg, the one cross-border broadcaster to the UK that had been able to restart operations after the war. The Luxembourg signal could only reach us after dark and even then it faded in and out. I was greatly influenced by radio probably because it was the number one media tool.

Television was a luxury item. I don't remember how old I was when we got our first TV, but I can recall the small set sitting in the corner of the front room. I often wondered why it was in the room we rarely used; perhaps there was nowhere else for it to go. The picture was in black and white, drizzled with electrical interference. I didn't watch much TV but was mesmerised by children's shows such as *Andy Pandy*, *The Woodentops*, *Rag, Tag and Bobtail* and *Muffin the Mule*.

The early morning milkman had already delivered the milk before we went out to play but there were lots more deliveries to come. What excitement when the pop man arrived with his van full of colourful soft drinks and fizzy pop. You washed out and returned your empty glass bottles to the pop man in return for money. I think it was around one penny a bottle at the time. I joined the queue of children with their empty bottles and returned home with a bottle of dandelion and burdock, soda water or lemonade.

The rag-and-bone man never failed to interrupt our games. He was a regular sight on the street when I was a young child and could be heard calling "Any old iron?" or "Rag bone" long before you saw him with his horse and cart. Times were still hard for many people and nothing was wasted or thrown away. Recycling was a way of life in the 1950s and 1960s and of course is returning today as we realise the need to protect the environment. The years of wartime austerity had taught people to make do and mend and not to waste a thing. Anything we thought the rag-and-bone man would take away was put to one side. He took anything he could sell on and played an important role in taking away unwanted material. I don't remember him coming beyond my early years.

At the outbreak of war most of the younger rag-and-bone men were called up to serve in the armed forces and the older men transferred to work elsewhere for the war effort. But after the war they did reappear briefly, mainly using vans although some clung to their horses. Today we have council rubbish tips and car boot sales for our unwanted household articles, a service that rag-and-bone men had provided for hundreds of years.

The coalman could guarantee an audience of noisy children during the school holidays. We didn't get too close as he was rather scary. He was "as black as the ace of spades", as people would say then, from all the coal dust, but had paler rings around his eyes where he had rubbed the dust away. He wore a thick leather sleeveless jacket to protect his shoulders and back when carrying the heavy bags of coal. I can still remember the smell of the coal as he tipped it from the outside through the trapdoor into our cellar.

We all had a dustbin to collect the dust from our coal fires. Household dustbins were made of galvanised steel, small by today's standard but there was little packaging to be disposed of in those days. The bin was collected from the back of the house by the dustman, hoisted onto his back, carried to the dustcart, emptied then returned.

We liked to play at the front of the YMCA building at the bottom of the street but rarely ventured to the top of the street where Tilly lived. She was an old lady who lived alone in a dark house. Her face was grey and deeply wrinkled with an angry expression and she was always dressed from top to toe in black. She didn't seem to like kids as she snarled at us, exposing her rotten teeth. She had lots of cats and when they had kittens she would put them in a bag and drown them. We never went too near her house as we thought she was a witch and were afraid she'd put a spell on us.

A gang of us would start bonfire progging in the October half-term holiday. The whole street would contribute stuff to burn. The bonfire was built on spare land at the bottom of the street. As soon as it got dark on November 5 the pile of timber was lit which would bring neighbours and people from the village. Everyone was welcome. Adults used to do baked potatoes and chestnuts on the fire. I remember the smell of spuds roasting on the edge of the fire; they usually ended up burnt on the outside and a bit raw on the inside. Lots of fireworks would be going off, rockets, sparklers and bangers. If it was a weekend we could stay out late. There was no such thing as organised bonfires in those days.

CHAPTER 11

Saturdays and Sundays

Weekends had their own routine. So I'd sometimes come from school on Friday and change into a cotton knee-length dress and a home-knitted cardigan ready to go to the youth club at the YMCA building. It was held in a large room on the first floor and was soon packed full of young kids dancing around to loud music. I never understood why Dad came to meet me when it had finished as I'd only a short walk home. Perhaps he didn't want me to find John O'Connor slumped in the ginnel.

Saturdays gave us a chance to do things as a family. It was the day for Mum to take off her pinny and dress up. I hardly recognised her wearing make-up, a pretty outfit and high-heeled shoes. Mum kept her best shoes in a cupboard in her bedroom. I remember finding them as a young child while snooping around and spent many hours tottering about on them. It was good to be able to spend some time with Dad. We didn't see much of him during the week as he worked long hours at Dean, Smith & Grace, a British manufacturer of lathes and milling machines in Keighley. I must have been around eight or nine when we started going to the 'pictures'. No one referred to going to the 'cinema' in those days. Saturday morning pictures became popular as a treat. Even if you had a television at home, the screens were tiny and the choice of programmes was small. We had to travel to Keighley where there were lots of picture houses to choose from. As the railway station in Cullingworth had now closed we had to travel to Keighley by bus, which I didn't enjoy. The journey was only ten minutes by train compared to the 20-minute grind on the bus travelling through Flappit Springs and Crossroads.

Church and Sunday school were the order of the day on Sundays. I had to wear my Sunday-best clothes, a dark-blue pleated skirt with matching long-sleeved jacket fastened with white mother of pearl buttons, clean white socks and polished black shoes. My unruly curly hair was brushed and neatly held in place with a large white ribbon. Mum took me to the Baptist church in the village but rarely stayed herself; lots of children went to church in the 1950s so I wasn't alone. The church had large wooden pews and an organ and a place for the Minister to stand at the front. The church was always packed with elderly women in the congregation, who liked to keep a close eye on the kids. I daydreamed my way through the sermon. What was the Minister talking about? It went way above my head. The only respite was singing the hymns. I remember an old lady talking to me as we were leaving the church: "Now if you do what Jesus tells you, be good and work hard, he will answer all your prayers. You can ask him for help with anything." Her advice stuck in my mind over the next few years and I thought it was worth a try before sitting for the 11-plus. I'd behaved myself and worked hard at school so prayed for help with the exam. Sadly, it didn't work. Sunday school was more fun than church. It was like school but we only learnt about Jesus. We did drawings and paintings and sang Sunday school songs. We could often be heard singing: *I'm H-A-P-P-Y, Jesus, Friend of Little Children* and *I'll be a Sunbeam.* In December it was Christmas carols, such as *In the Bleak Midwinter* and *Away in a Manger.*

We always had a Sunday roast consisting of roasted meat, potatoes, Yorkshire pudding, vegetables and gravy at lunchtime. I often thought I was sent to church and Sunday school to get me out of the house while Mum prepared the meal. Although most of the leftover food from our Sunday roast formed the basis of meals served on other days of the week, there was always some meat kept for Mrs Carter's dog in Lodge Street. I didn't like her bulldog; it was so ugly with its flat face. I was glad when we got Rex, a cross-breed terrier. He was a much nicer dog and I didn't have to take the leftovers to Mrs Carter's anymore.

Sunday evenings were dull, mainly at the thought of going back to school the next day. I recall reluctantly sitting on the wooden dining chair positioned in the centre of the kitchen while my mother covered my shoulders with a towel, pulled the ribbon out of my hair and grabbed the nit comb. With my head bent over a sheet of newspaper, she started raking through my hair in search of nits. I didn't understand what it was all about but knew we shouldn't go to school with them. Would Mum be pleased if she found some? I stared at the newspaper in anticipation, waiting for the nits to fall. When she was satisfied I was nit free I was given a spoonful of malt and cod liver oil before having my weekly bath. We were lucky having a bathroom as lots of families still had to have a wash in a tin bath in front of the fire. Helen remembers the days when we only had a sink and toilet in the house and she went to Grandma Field's house to have her weekly bath. Grandma and Grandad Field lived in Prospect House at the top of Lodge Street at the time. I was too young to remember them living there but it sounded such fun. Helen and my older cousins would often tell me about the house and the happy times they spent playing in the orchard, often getting told off by Grandma for misbehaving.

CHAPTER 12

Coal Fires

Our house was freezing in the winter. Apart from a small plug-in electric fire, coal was our only source of heating. The kitchen fire was lit most days during the winter. We were allowed to set the fire from an early age but not light it until we were older. I enjoyed rolling the newspaper for the first layer, then piling on the sticks before putting the coal on the top. Collecting the coal from the cellar was a different story. There was a single electric bulb at the top of the cellar steps which didn't give out much light. So we had to walk carefully down the stone steps into the dark, cold cellar, then shovel up the coal and carry the heavy bucket back.

There were also fireplaces in the bedrooms, and a fire might be lit if one of us was ill in bed. When it was cold and frosty, icicles would form on the inside of the windows of the back bedroom that Jane and I shared, and Mum would plug the electric fire in for a while before we went to bed. Hot water bottles were put in our twin beds to take the chill off the sheets. Extra coverings were found if it was very cold and Mum tucked us into bed so tightly we could hardly move under the weight of the blankets and bedspread. It would often be so cold you could see your breath in the air. If it was raining, we'd often fall asleep to the sound of dripping water coming through our bedroom ceiling and into the bucket. Jane's bed was near the window wall of the bedroom, mine was against the opposite wall which had a recess where we kept our books and some toys. A curtain went across the recess to keep things tidy. Mum would sometimes read us a bedtime story. She was an avid reader and could quickly get lost in a book. I loved listening to stories about her childhood and often asked her to tell me about her friend Ivy who walked about trailing a big heavy bag behind her.

The coal fires gave out a lot of smoke which would increase as the chimney got blocked up with soot. So it was essential to have the chimney swept once or twice a year. If Dad didn't have time to do it we had to send for the chimney sweep. What a palaver it was. Mum would cover everything in dust sheets and hope the sweep would come early as the cleaning up afterwards took ages. The chimney sweep always looked miserable as he arrived with his brushes, sacks, shovels and cloths. He would drape a large cloth in front of the fireplace before Jane and I would run to the top of the garden and wait for the brush coming out of the top of the chimney. He would then pull the brush back down creating a deal of soot for him to shovel up and put into sacks. Mum joined us in the garden while the dust settled before the major operation of cleaning up. She swept and brushed up loose soot from the floor, the ceiling and walls. Then she set to with a bucket of soapy water. If a film of dust remained, cleaning had to be repeated until the room was spotless. Everything was back in its place by teatime.

It's hard to believe that children were widely used as chimney sweeps for about 200 years and what they had to endure was the stuff of nightmares. The practice was finally stopped in 1875 following the death of George Brewster, a 12-year-old chimney sweep who became stuck in a flue at Fulbourn Hospital, Cambridge. He was rescued but died shortly afterwards. George was the last child apprentice chimney sweep to die on the job.

It was good to huddle round the fire on a cold winter's night. Heavy curtains hung behind the outside doors to help keep out the draughts. Mum would be listening to the radio or quietly reading. Dad might be checking his football pools or darning his socks. You didn't throw away socks just because they had a hole in them in those days. I loved to watch my father putting the sock over what looked like a big wooden mushroom. Then he'd thread a darning needle and off he went. He always did a good job but the thread didn't always match his socks.

CHAPTER 13

Christmas

Mum and Dad always made a big effort to ensure that Christmas was a very special occasion for all the family. It was spent in the front room with Dad in charge of the decorations. The artificial tree was taken out of its box and decorated with baubles and lights with a fairy stuck on the top. Jane and I would help but I imagine we rather got in the way. The lights always caused problems and Dad invariably had to patiently fiddle about with them for ages to get them to work. Colourful paper decorations were pinned across the ceiling with a large paper bell hanging down in the centre.

The week before Christmas was busy. Dad only had Christmas Day and Boxing day off work so Mum was rushing around getting the house ready and buying the food in. Children were busy going to parties. An annual Christmas party was held at the Conservative Club in the village, for the children, grandchildren and relations of members. I wasn't keen on parties but enjoyed going because my cousins and friends were there. We had lots of fun and games, free food and drinks, ice-creams, sweets and crisps. Then Santa would visit with presents. One year I recognised Santa; he was a man I knew in the village. I rushed over to tell my mother he wasn't the real Santa and she was unable to convince me otherwise. We also had a party at school before breaking up for the Christmas holidays. It was good fun with lots of food but Santa didn't come. Even the teachers seemed to enjoy it.

On Christmas Eve after Dad had put a mince pie and a glass of sherry out for Santa, he would meet Uncle Clifford in the Conservative Club for a Christmas drink. He always came home late in a happy mood. Jane and I would venture up to bed early and toss and turn for ages, too excited to go to sleep. Morning arrived and we dressed quickly in the freezing bedroom before running downstairs to see what Santa had brought us. In those days there wasn't the pressure for parents to buy the latest toy for their demanding offspring. We didn't get the amount of presents that kids get today, just one present each from immediate family plus the odd gift from friends and neighbours.

Dad was always up before us and we were greeted by roaring fires in both downstairs rooms. It felt really cosy. Dad's efforts had paid off; the decorations looked lovely and to his relief the Christmas tree lights were twinkling brightly. I remember the Christmas that 'Patsy' arrived. I had asked Santa for a dolls' pram and to my delight there it stood, a beautiful brown pram with a bright blue interior. Excitedly I ran over and peered inside to find a black doll with a hard plastic head, soft body, big brown eyes that opened and closed, long eyelashes and black tightly curled short hair. She was wearing brown trousers, a yellow jacket and a matching yellow and brown hat that Grandma Clark had knitted for her. She was perfect. I almost forgot about the pillowcase filled with my other presents. It must have been a struggle financially for my parents to give us the presents we wanted, but they always did. Mum told me many years later that the pram was second-hand. I couldn't have liked it any more had it have been a new one. Jane and I were always appreciative of all the presents we received.

My parents cooked the Christmas dinner together, putting the turkey in the oven early and then chopping vegetables. If we were able to tear ourselves away from our presents, we would help with setting the table and washing up. The table was set in the front room, with the best tablecloth, crockery and cutlery; it looked very posh. Dad proudly carved the turkey, which we ate with all the trimmings, potatoes and a selection of fresh vegetables, followed by a large helping of Christmas pudding. There was hardly time to wash up and for the meal to be digested before the table was reset for tea – a buffet of cold meats, pork pie and salad, plus trifle, cake and mince pies. It was such a busy day with relatives, friends and neighbours popping in. We were all exhausted by the end of the day.

As for Patsy, she was my favourite doll and was well looked after. I would play with her for hours, bathing her, feeding her and taking her out for walks in my dolls' pram, stopping off to let the neighbours admire her. She eventually began to look worse for wear as she lost an eyelash and the colour of her body started to fade due to all the baths she'd had. I still loved Patsy and she remained in the family long after I'd stopped playing with dolls.

CHAPTER 14

Seaside Fun

Summers of years gone by have so many memories for me: seaside holidays, days out, funfairs, picnics. The great British seaside holiday came into its heyday in the post-war years and had become affordable to many thanks to the 1938 Holidays with Pay Act. The destinations of choice depended largely on where you lived. Mum and Dad saved hard throughout the year so we could go away in the summer. Dad was always ready for our seaside holiday; apart from bank holidays he only had two weeks off a year. It was a busy time as many industrial towns like Keighley had holiday weeks when local factories like Dean, Smith & Grace would shut down for maintenance and all the workers would take their annual leave at the same time.

In the 1950s and 1960s it was unusual for families to holiday abroad. For us the destination was Scarborough, Britain's first ever seaside resort and the largest on the Yorkshire coast. The most striking feature of the town's geography is the high rocky promontory pointing eastward into the North Sea with the 11th-century ruins of Scarborough castle perched on the top. The promontory divides the seafront into two bays, North and South. We always stayed in South Bay, which was the site of the medieval settlement and harbour which form the old town, and is the main tourist area with a sandy beach, cafes, amusement arcades, candyfloss stalls, seafood shacks, theatres and entertainment. North Bay is the more peaceful end of the resort and is home to Peasholm Park with its Chinese-themed lake and mystical gardens.

At that time we didn't have a car so had to travel by coach. We took a large, brown leather suitcase with us. It was packed so full that we had to sit on the top to close the lid so Dad could lock it. Auntie Linda's family and Uncle Clifford's family often joined us. The coach was always full of families eager to escape from their daily lives. The journey took the best part of the day and we were relieved when we arrived at Mrs Hartley's boarding house.

We spent most of our days at Scarborough on the beach. Soon after breakfast we rushed around getting together our swimsuits, towels, buckets and spades. And off we went, Dad picking up a newspaper and a packet of flags to adorn our sandcastles on the way. We tried to get to the beach early, as we needed plenty of space for all the family. Deckchairs could be rented for the day or half day; we usually got ours for the day. It was fun watching the adults trying to figure out how to put them up. They didn't always get it right as the deckchairs would sometimes collapse when they were sat on. It wasn't long before the beach was full. There was often a breeze and you would find the adults sheltering behind windbreaks, while the children were happily playing. Although most of my cousins were older than me, we all had fun, at very little cost, playing ball, making sandcastles, paddling in the sea and jumping over the waves. I enjoyed running down to the shore to explore the rock pools as the tide was going out. They were full of amazing sea-life; it was so exciting seeing the bizarre and fascinating creatures.

My cousins kept a close eye on me so I didn't get stung by jellyfish while picking up rocks and inspecting seaweed.

I will never forget the ghastly elasticated swimsuit that stuck to my skin when I went in the sea. The bikini became very popular with women in the 1950s but Mum never wore one. She wore a swimsuit and Dad wore his swimming trunks and T-shirt if the weather was warm. I often wondered why some of the men were fully dressed on the beach with a white knotted handkerchief on their heads. It was such a treat going for a donkey ride or sitting on the sand with a large group of kids watching the Punch and Judy show. It was important that we went home with a suntan to show Rhoda next door proof that we had been on holiday. Unfortunately, sunburn wasn't considered a health risk and suntan lotion wasn't available like it is today. Mum would often treat my painful sunburn with calamine lotion. One year my sunburn was so bad, Mum bought me a new swimsuit to cheer me up.

The seafront was always busy. Dad found the amusement arcades hard to resist. Mum wasn't happy as she disapproved of gambling and we were given a small handful of pennies to play on the machines and told, "There are no more pennies once they've gone". We never stayed long in the arcades and rarely left with more money than we started with. The shops were full of people buying sweets, ice-cream, buckets and spades, and postcards. If you didn't send postcards to grandparents and other family members you were in trouble – bearing in mind we didn't have mobile phones and e-mails back then. I remember one day being distracted by a screeching of brakes as we walked along the front. It was the Williamson family from Cullingworth arriving on holiday in their motorbike and sidecar. Mrs Williamson, looking windswept, was clinging onto her husband for dear life. Mr Williamson was his usual jolly self while their children, Susan and David, looked none too pleased, squashed in the sidecar surrounded by luggage. After extracting themselves from the vehicle, we arranged to meet on the beach. We decided it would be fun to dig a big hole and bury David in the sand, with only his head visible. We were in fits of laughter watching him wriggling around, trying to get out. We left him struggling for a while before releasing him. Waving farewell to the Williamson family as they started their journey home, I felt grateful my dad hadn't got a sidecar on his motorbike.

If we needed anything from the town we had a ride on the Central Tramway, the oldest surviving cliff railway in the country, established in 1881. It has two tracks running between Marine Parade in the centre of Scarborough and Foreshore Road on South Bay beach. It was a steep climb up to the town and although there were steps beside the tramway, we liked to save our legs after the long walk along the front. The tram at the top station set off at the same time as the one at the bottom station, passing halfway. We would wave at the passengers in the other tram as we passed. I enjoyed the journey up but the journey back down could be rather scary as a young child.

One of the highlights of our holiday was a visit to Peasholm Park. People would travel from the centre of town and along the seafront on buses which terminated at the Corner Cafe. The cafe was a big part of North Bay at the time, but has now been replaced by apartments and shops. A short walk from the beach took us into the park with its lake, tree walk, mystical gardens and mini-golf. We were never short of something to do, from enjoying the sights and grabbing an ice-cream, to hiring a boat or feeding the ducks and squirrels.

Evenings on holiday were a special time. We all looked smart as we walked out especially Mum wearing make-up and a new figure-hugging calf-length dress and high-heeled shoes. Buying new shoes always seemed a palaver for my mother. She had to break them in before they were comfortable enough to wear outdoors. This entailed walking about the house in them until they no longer rubbed her feet and caused blisters. Cousin Joyce took the same size shoes, so was able to help with the breaking in process. Dad would also look smart for the evenings in his shirt, trousers and highly polished shoes. Helen and my cousins Janet, Jean and Joyce were all in their teens and looked very grown-up in their pretty clothes and broken-in new shoes. Mum always made sure Jane and I looked pretty too in our dresses and sandals.

Summer evenings found families strolling along the pier with the smell of fish and chips, hot dogs, candyfloss and seaweed filling the air. If it was a flat, calm sea we would cruise the coastline on one of the pleasure steamers. "Do you want to go on the *Regal Lady* or the *Coronia*?" Dad would ask. Both boats were used to bring soldiers back from Dunkirk in World War Two and it was amazing how these two vessels had survived the ravages of the war.

On the last day of our holiday it was customary for us to go for a knickerbocker glory. This sundae, which came in a tall cone-shaped glass, consisted of raspberry jelly, chunks of tinned peach and different flavoured ice-cream scattered with crushed nuts and topped with a glazed cherry. You ate it with a long shiny spoon and it took ages to get all the bits of peach from the bottom of the glass.

We continued to holiday in Scarborough for many years, moving from staying in the boarding house to renting a terrace house which was big enough for all the family. We had to take our own sheets and towels but the rent was cheap. There was never a dull moment with lots of comings and goings from family and friends. Grandma Field came on holiday with us several times. She had never been to the seaside before then. The house was really convenient, just cross the road, run down the steep stone steps and there was the beach. As Helen and my older cousins grew older, they went their separate ways for holidays.

The true seaside holiday had everything as a child. Playing on the windswept beach, having fun and adventure with sand all over me, it was a time and a place where you could let your imagination run away with you.

Molly paddling in the sea

*Playing with Susan & David Williamson on the beach
in Scarborough*

*Mum & me on the left with Auntie Linda & Cousin Christopher
in his one-piece swimsuit!*

Sister Helen (left) Me & Mum on Scarborough beach

Sister Helen (left) with Sister Jane

From left Sister Jane, Cousin Jean, Cousin Janet & Me

Me with Mum

*Dad (left) with Mum, sister Jane & me walking along
Scarborough Pier*

CHAPTER 15

On My Bike

During the 1950s parents were more trusting, yet less permissive, with their kids. Daily care activities, discipline and communication with children was a woman's job – the trend towards dads as caregivers hadn't even begun to take shape. Parents would allow their children to explore without restrictions, trusting them to keep themselves safe instead of constantly hovering over them in a protective manner. Freedoms such as riding a bike to a friend's house or playing in the park without a mum or dad present were common.

I must have been around the age of nine when I was allowed to venture further afield but Mum or a member of my family were always around when I came home from school. However, some children did walk home on their own, often letting themselves into the house with the door key left hanging on a string inside the letterbox. My friend Susan Ingham lived in a large detached house in Bents Lane, a remote area near Goit Stock. As her mum worked full time and there was no bus service to her house, she often had to walk home from school. I enjoyed walking with her on a summer's evening. On leaving the village you were surrounded by open fields, trees, and several farmhouses with animals roaming around. It was a long walk and took ages as we stopped at Goit Stock to watch the waterfall, before walking up the hill to her house. Susan's dad, a quietly spoken, frail-looking man who rarely left the house, was always in the kitchen preparing tea for when her mum got in from work. We didn't have much time at the house before I had to walk all the way back. I would be in bother if I was late home for tea.

It was a surprise the day my bike arrived – adult sized with a horizontal crossbar, hard saddle and dropped handlebars, passed on from Cousin Joyce. Not a suitable choice for a young girl wearing a dress! How was I going to get on the bike? And how was I going to lift my leg over the crossbar without showing my knickers? How could I learn to ride it if I couldn't even reach the saddle? Hopefully I would soon grow into it. But I wasn't going to be beaten, so off I went to the Rec, a busy meeting place for kids in the village. The Rec had a park at the bottom with a slide, swings and roundabout, and a large, grassed area leading up to the tennis courts and bowling green. It was the ideal place to learn to cycle. And there, with the help of my friends and many hours of practice and numerous falls and bruises, I learnt to ride my bike. There was no dad teaching me while holding onto the saddle and no helmet worn back then.

Uncle Clifford's family lived in a small terrace house overlooking the Rec. It was smaller than our house, with only a kitchen and sitting room downstairs. Cousin Jean thought we were posh because we had a best room in our house. I often called to see them. Auntie Nora was a petite Irish lady who always made me feel welcome. "Come in, Molly. We'll have a biting on," she'd say. The "biting on" was a snack to keep you going until your next meal. Uncle

Clifford would often be in the garden or reading the paper. Mum spoke very fondly about her older brother, who had played a large part in her growing up. My cousins were close in age to each other and all attended the grammar school. Janet and Jean were very studious and often found studying, with their sister Joyce distracting them. She was the tomboy of the family who would rather be outside than spending too much time on homework. Janet had been a sickly young child. Grandma Field had been concerned as she was always tired and often lay on the couch after school while the other kids were outside playing. The school doctor diagnosed a severe heart defect when she had her school leaving medical examination. How had she managed to pass the 11-plus? The school prayed for her on the day she had major surgery. It wasn't known what the outcome would be, but she made a full recovery and led a full, healthy life.

The bike opened up a whole new life of freedom for me. I was soon cycling on the main roads and visiting friends. Andrea Kemp, the posh girl famous for dropping a penny into Miss Johns' honey, invited me to play at her house. Heart beating fast and pedalling hard I cycled up Station Road, along Turf Lane and up Haworth Road to Coldspring House. I couldn't believe my eyes cycling through the gateway and along the cobbled stone drive towards a very grand house. We played outside for hours in the surrounding fields or in the barn. If it was raining, we went indoors. The house was huge. The hallway was almost as big as our house with a wide central stairway leading up to the bedrooms. Andrea had a large bedroom which she didn't have to share with her sister. She kept white mice in a cage and when their numbers increased, she sold them. Mum wasn't pleased the day I arrived home with two white mice.

CHAPTER 16

Visiting

We rarely saw Auntie Ada's family as they didn't live in the village and never joined us on holiday. So Mum looked forward to a day's outing to visit them. Jane and I would be smartly dressed before setting off. The bus terminus was only a short walk to the bottom of the street and as Grandma Field was now living a few doors up from Auntie Linda in Lodge Street we could pop and see them both before the bus arrived. Auntie Linda had a clear view of the bus stop and on a sunny day would often be found sitting outside her front door, dressed in her pinny and scarf, observing the buses coming and going, and having a natter with passers-by while Uncle Albert was running errands for the neighbours.

We joined the orderly queue in good time as the bus only stopped long enough to allow passengers on and off. We were soon on our way to Haworth. When I was growing up every bus had a conductor as well as a driver. I remember bus conductors being smartly dressed in dark-blue uniforms and wearing a badge. They were in charge, monitoring safety and signalling to their driver by ringing a bell when it was safe to pull away from the bus stop. Once the passengers were all settled in their seats, the conductor moved up and down the bus selling tickets. If the bus was crowded he had to squeeze past the standing passengers. We were taught at an early age to give our seats to old people and ladies with young children if they couldn't find a seat. I watched the conductor collect the money in a pouch slung over his neck and shoulders, then pull out the ticket from a rack before putting it in the ticket machine to punch a hole in it.

We soon reached our stop opposite Haworth train station, and the three of us would walk over the station bridge and up the cobbles to Ivy Bank Lane. Steep stone steps led up to Auntie Ada's smart Victorian terrace house. The large hallway led to the front room where Uncle Gilbert could often be heard playing the piano. He was a slim, dark-haired man with a surly character and tendency to be quite brusque. I never really liked him. He was a chess champion and would sometimes have a game of draughts with me. I never won but he said I was a good player and should keep practising. Uncle Gilbert was a painter and decorator and would often be in the house wearing his white overalls splattered with paint. No wonder the kitchen had a paint smell.

Auntie Ada was an attractive lady with a warm smile. She was always pleased to see us. Cousins Brian and James were much older than me, so I never knew them well. Marlene was only a year older than me but while I was still enjoying being an innocent, carefree child wearing socks and sandals and climbing trees, she was dressing much older and doing more grown-up things. I recall her proudly showing me a pair of new heeled shoes her dad had bought her, before wrapping them in tissue paper and placing them back in the box. Marlene had more or less anything she wanted but she wasn't a happy child. Years later Mum told me that Auntie Ada was in an abusive marriage and would often leave her husband to stay with Grandma. But she always went back. In the 1950s divorce was relatively uncommon and often still frowned upon despite the liberation it offered many people trapped in loveless marriages.

The old adage that children should be seen and not heard came into play when visiting Auntie Millie. She was Grandma Field's sister, a rotund lady with short, white, wavy hair and a stern face. She always looked miserable; it was hard to believe she was Grandma's sister. Auntie Millie's house was always tidy with everything in its place and nothing out of place. I would sit still and only speak if spoken to. It was so boring with nothing to do but listen to the adult conversation and the clock loudly ticking on the chest of drawers behind me. It seemed customary back then to have a ticking clock in every room of the house. I was glad when it was time to leave.

A visit to Auntie Elsie and Uncle Harold was something we all enjoyed. They were a lovely couple who couldn't have children of their own but always made a big fuss of Jane and me. We usually visited on a Sunday so Dad could come with us. We had to travel to Keighley on the bus as Dad never got a sidecar for his motorbike. He did occasionally take me for a ride on it. In his strong Glaswegian accent he would say, "Jump oan th back o th bike n haud oan ticht lass" as he helped me climb aboard. I clung on to Dad tightly as we set off. It is hard to believe that wearing a motorcycle crash helmet didn't become compulsory until 1973. Auntie Elsie was a petite lady with short blonde hair and a lovely smile; she would have been a lovely mum. Uncle Harold was a smart man, tall and thin like a pelican. It was obvious he adored his wife. Auntie Elsie always made a special tea with more food than you could possibly eat. She was a good baker and we always had a selection of cakes, buns, scones, tarts and fruit pies to finish off with. I clearly remember one day we visited when I was struggling to remove my silver bracelets. Mum and Dad had bought me two bracelets when I was very young and I liked them so much I rarely took them off. I hadn't noticed they had become tight. I was in tears as the butter dish appeared and with my hand smothered in butter a lot of pulling and pushing went on to no avail. I had to eventually have the bracelets cut off. I was surprised when told Auntie Elsie and Uncle Harold weren't my proper auntie and uncle; they were friends of my parents. But it didn't make any difference to the relationship I had with them. Auntie Elsie would give me some pennies as we were leaving to buy some sweets to share with Jane.

These days a penny is an insignificant amount, but back then a penny for a child was a real treat. Spending money wasn't given like today – you had to earn it by helping with the daily chores. The sweet shop was a fascinating place. I can picture myself standing at the counter in Robertshaw's sweet shop making the agonising decision of how to spend my penny. I would stare at the huge glass jars filled with magical coloured sweets. There was such a vast choice: dolly mixtures, pineapple chunks, aniseed balls, fruit salad, jelly babies, spearmint chews, sherbet lemons, liquorice allsorts. Gobstoppers were huge balls of coloured layers that you sucked away, but they were quite costly as they were tuppence each. You could buy Barratt's sweet cigarettes, made of white sickly stuff with a red end, and pretend to be smoking. Mars Bars cost around four pence so if we wanted one we had to share it. Once you had chosen your sweets they were transferred into a small white paper bag and carried home carefully. I would often save my sweets to eat later.

CHAPTER 17

Delivery Girl

I rarely got the chance to spend much time with Dad, so would take every opportunity possible. He started work very early and from a young age I would hurry to put my dressing gown and slippers on before creeping quietly downstairs to join him for breakfast. On a cold, draughty morning he would have already lit the coal fire, but it wasn't always straight forward. I'd open the kitchen door to the sight of Dad standing in front of the fire holding a broadsheet newspaper up to the fireplace to draw the draught up the flue to get the fire to burn better, while muttering about the wind coming down the chimney or the damp coal. The process was effective but not always safe as the newspaper often caught fire. The kitchen soon felt warm and the fire looked lovely with its multi-coloured flames dancing above the coals and glowing coves between the pieces of fuel. It was good to have a chat, just Dad and me. But breakfast finished, he was soon jumping on his motorbike and waving as he set off to work. We were lucky as we had a back boiler behind the fireplace which provided hot water when the fire was lit. It was much nicer to have a wash in hot water on a winter's morning.

The entire street took pride in their gardens and come springtime the neighbours were all out busy digging and weeding. The trees were turning various shades of green and the spring flowers were bursting open. Mr and Mrs Peacock had the most beautiful tulips providing a blanket of vivid colour. Mum thought very highly of Mr and Mrs Peacock, a retired couple who had two grown-up, married daughters, Renee and Rosie. We didn't see much of their daughters who both lived down south and worked as Nursing Sisters. Mum often told me how well they had done.

Dad's garden was his pride and joy. I can picture myself helping him with the regimental planting of the vegetables, in true Percy Thrower fashion: potatoes, carrots, runner beans, peas, radishes and lettuce. I enjoyed watering the plants and watching them grow until they were ready to eat. Fresh peas from the garden were one of my favourites and I often got the job of helping to shell them. I remember struggling to snap the stem and pull the thick string of fibre along the length of the pea pod and push the peas into a dish. I couldn't resist eating some along the way and often got told off as not all the peas ended up in the dish. Our garden was a blaze of vibrant colour in the summer and Dad would sell bunches of flowers to the villagers. The orders started coming in fast so I had to step in and be the delivery girl. Dad would carefully select the flowers with my help, admiring each dahlia or hydrangea before he cut the stalk. After removing all the creepy-crawlies, I'd carefully wrap the flowers in newspaper and off I went to deliver them. I must have walked miles around the village. Everyone was delighted with their flowers and I always got some spending money.

Unfortunately, the flower delivery season was soon over so I had to think of some other way to make money. What about shopping? Cullingworth was well served with a variety of shops and I sometimes popped to the local shops for Mum on Saturday mornings. So would it be an idea to ask the neighbours if they wanted any shopping doing? The numbers grew quickly and I soon had a good little business going on. Off I'd go armed with a number of shopping lists plus money and needed to make several trips to carry all the stuff. Saturdays were always busy. Binns grocery shop would be queued to the door but, being a very nosey child, I didn't mind the wait as I listened in to the local gossip. My last port of call was Mitchell's bakery shop. Situated at the bottom of Mill Street it was on my way home. My mouth watered at the smell of freshly baked bread as I admired the display of cakes, buns and fruit tarts. I imagined Mum in front of the fire with a thick slice of white bread stuck on the end of the toasting fork. When ready, the toast was thickly spread with butter that trickled down your chin as you ate it. The shopkeepers were very helpful sorting all the money out so I didn't get confused. It took ages but the sums I received from the neighbours for doing their shopping boosted my income.

I don't know why I have no recollection of food rationing and ration books, as I must have been around six years old when it ended. Mum often spoke about the different coloured ration books that contained coupons and explained that the colour of your book was very important as it made sure you got the right amount and type of food needed for your health. Most adults had a buff-coloured ration book. Pregnant women, nursing mothers and children under five had a green book, as they had first choice of fruit, a daily pint of milk and a double supply of eggs. The blue book was for children up to 16 years of age as it was felt important they had fruit, the full meat ration and half a pint of milk a day. Children must have been overjoyed on February 5, 1953, when sweet rationing ended. Food rationing ended at midnight on July 4 the following year.

Mum bought fresh eggs from Mr and Mrs Brown, an elderly couple who lived in a smart terrace house at the top of our street. Mrs Brown was an attractive lady with short white hair, striking pale-blue eyes and a warm smile. Mr Brown was a slight man, his complexion pale and pasty, his greying hair carefully combed to hide the fact that it was thinning. They were both friendly, well- known and respected in the village. I enjoyed collecting the eggs for Mum, often staying a while and having a chat. They were like grandparents to me.

It was a warm sunny day with not a cloud in the sky as I happily set off with my small wicker basket to collect the eggs. I had to pass Helen's house on the way. She was now living opposite Tilly and her cats in a small one-up, one-down terrace house at the top of Mill Street with her husband Brian. The house was much smaller than ours with a living room and pantry downstairs, a steep stone staircase leading to a bedroom upstairs. Like many houses in the 1950s it didn't have a bathroom; the outside toilet was further down the street, round the corner. You had to take your own roll of hard Izal loo paper with the scent of disinfectant or use the squares of old newspaper strung on a nail. The toilet was used in all weathers, rain or shine. But chamber pots were used inside the house, particularly during the night, when they were kept under the bed.

The chickens were roaming around pecking the grass and clucking as I arrived at the Browns' house for the eggs. I enthusiastically knocked on the door. Mr Brown looked surprised to see me as he answered the door. "Oh Molly, I wondered who was calling. I gather you want some eggs," he said, glancing at my basket. I smiled and nodded as he opened the door to let me in. I soon started to feel uncomfortable as he locked the door behind me and slipped the key in his trouser pocket. He seemed very quiet as I followed him into the sitting room. The room was very tidy as usual but felt cold and empty. "Is Mrs Brown in?" I asked. "No, she's gone out shopping and won't be back until later," he replied. He barely spoke as he took the basket into the kitchen and carefully filled it with a dozen eggs. I was standing in the sitting room when he returned. His face somehow looked different and without speaking he put my basket on a chest of drawers and, before I could blink, he grabbed my arms and shoved me against the wall, effectively pinning me against the wall with his body. I was a happy, innocent child around nine or ten years old, unaware what was happening. But I knew it was wrong and I was very frightened. He continued to hold me tightly as he pressed his dry lips against mine and put his hands underneath my clothes. My heart was beating fast and tears welled up in my eyes as I was unable to move. I could smell his breath. It went on for a while before I was able to scream, wriggle and kick him. He eventually let go of me saying he would only open the door if I promised never to tell anyone and that included my sister Helen.

Back home Mum was worried; she knew something untoward must have happened. I tried to tell her but couldn't. I kept my promise. I didn't visit the house again. What happened that day continued to affect me up until leaving home. I would make sure he wasn't around before going out or coming home and could recognise his footsteps as he walked past our front door in the evening on his way to the Friendly Inn. The last time I saw him was years later when I was on my way to visit my parents who had moved to a bungalow in the village. I was proudly pushing my daughter Jacqueline in her pram when I came face to face with Mr Brown. I didn't immediately recognise him as he looked so old and frail. The memories of that day came flooding back as I turned and walked away. I saw that confused, frightened little girl again. I could see it, feel it, taste it, hear it and it hurt. But I never blamed myself. I was shaking and felt angry. Why had I never told anyone? Would anyone have believed me? Did Mrs Brown wonder why I stopped visiting? Did he abuse other children? I never told any of my family until recently. It's hard to believe how hidden and under-credited this taboo subject was back then.

CHAPTER 18

Free to Roam

The summer of 1959 was a long spell of blazing sunshine. Now aged 11, I had left primary school and was enjoying spending the school holidays with my friends before starting secondary school. We were now given a great amount of personal freedom. Parents trusted us to go out together, to make our own decisions and to make and learn from our own mistakes. We roamed freely and ventured further afield, leaving home in the morning with a packed lunch; the only rule was to be back for tea. A small group of us would often set off from the village and walk to Goit Stock. Surrounded by trees, fields, woodlands and a wide variety of flowers, it was a popular place to visit as a child. There was so much to enjoy, walking through the woodlands, along the stream, paddling, climbing trees and watching the wildlife. We spent a lot of time at the waterfalls, located in the secluded Goit Stock wood. We had to be careful as the paths were unsurfaced and rocky. The bottom pool has the largest falls and the top one is shallower and slightly less shaded. I was mesmerised watching the waterfall as it wistfully wound around the rocks, hiding from the sparkling summer sun, the light-blue and greyish colours turning white and frothy as they hit the pool. The air was cool and crisp, smelling of fresh water, wet leaves and newly cut grass. It was magical.

The world then without mobile phones, internet or fancy gadgets, gave us more time with friends, more opportunities to exercise and to develop better communication and social skills. Life in general was much less competitive than today.

As Jane was almost five years old, we were able to spend more time together. I would take her shopping and we would play games. We enjoyed going with Mum for a picnic in the Four Fields. "Pop and ask Grandma if she'd like to come with us while I'm making some sandwiches," Mum would say. "It's only a short walk so she should be able to manage it. It's a shame for her to miss such a lovely day." Grandma, sitting indoors, would quickly remove her pinny and put her scarf and shoes on. We soon set off with our picnic basket, a large blanket to sit on and a ball for Jane and me to play with. It was a real treat for Grandma as we shared our picnic in the sunshine. I spent ages showing Jane how to make daisy chains. "Only pick the ones with long stalks," I kept telling her as she grabbed them in handfuls. I had to show her how to split the stalk with her thumbnail about half-way down its length, then thread the stalk of another daisy through this hole. We would keep going until we had a really long daisy chain. It kept us occupied for quite some time making necklaces, bracelets, rings and crowns.

I recall having sleepless nights, tossing and turning at the thought of starting secondary school. Fortunately, Marilynne and I were firm friends and would be travelling to school together. Marilynne was a petite girl with short brown hair neatly framing her pretty face. She had a bubbly character, always happy and smiling. I loved visiting Marilynne's house with the brightly coloured fruit shop at the front and a cosy living room and kitchen at the back. Her maternal grandma, Nan, lived with them and was always busy pottering about. It was a hive of activity when the shop was open and such a happy household.

During the summer holiday I needed kitting out with my school uniform. Jane was starting primary school at the same time, but back then state primary schools didn't normally have uniforms. Mum must have been relieved she didn't have two uniforms to buy as they worked out quite expensive. I can picture myself happily going to O S Wains schoolwear shop in Bingley to buy all the items on the list in readiness for moving into my new school in September. The first and second-year girls wore V-necked, burgundy gymslips with matching ties. A gymslip is a sleeveless tunic, more commonly known as a pinafore dress. Boys wore short trousers. In your third year, girls moved on to skirts, and boys to long trousers. We also needed white blouses, white T-shirts for PE, white socks and a gabardine school coat. The school blazer was optional. One of my tasks over the school holidays was learning to tie a tie. Dad tried to teach me but I found the knot very confusing and it took hours of practice before I got the hang of it. Under the gymslip we had to wear thick navy knickers. These were the least favourite item of uniform, being huge, baggy creations with elastic sewn around the legs. Mum also bought me a leather satchel for my schoolbooks, pens and pencils, and a duffel bag for PE and swimming days.

CHAPTER 19

Big School

A hot day in early September found Jane and me anxiously getting ready for our first day at school. Mum made sure we had finished breakfast and were washed and dressed in plenty of time. Sporting my smart new gymslip, white blouse and tie, I closed the door behind me and briskly walked, with my satchel slung over my shoulder, down the street to the bus stop. I was in emotional turmoil, excited, nervous, scared, and filled with anticipation and curiosity. This was, after all, the first day at big school. I was relieved to see Marilynne had already joined the short queue of sleepy-looking new-intake kids. The older children were starting later in the day to give us a chance to settle in. The bus arrived on time, we all jumped on and were soon trundling down the steep cobbled "Twines" road on our way to school.

Bingley Secondary Modern School was a large, single-storey brick building with a tall clock tower. I felt overwhelmed looking at these new surroundings. Being a quiet, under-confident child, how was I going to cope? I was almost in tears. Mum had reassuringly said, "The first day is always the hardest, but you'll soon get used to it." But going from being the leaders of our last school to the youngest of this school wasn't going to be easy. We slowly walked towards the school playground and looked at all the other kids. Most were in groups, chatting and smiling. We joined a bunch of newbies from our school, anxiously waiting for the bell. Marilynne and I weren't in the same class but arranged to meet up at dinnertime. The corridors were like a maze with anxious children trying to find their classrooms. After a few wrong turnings we eventually found where we needed to be.

It was a large room with sunlight streaming through the window, the desks arranged in classic rows with the teacher's desk at the front, the blackboard behind her dominating the room. We all sat quietly at our desks. I don't recall my first, class teacher but remember being told the classroom rules and regulations and what we would be doing the rest of the school year. I kept staring at the large clock above the blackboard: it was the cruellest of all mechanisms, moving at a snail's pace. Will this morning ever end? My mind soon started wandering as I remembered progressing from writing with a pencil to a dipping pen when I was around seven years old. Old school desks had a little hole in them for a pot of ink. Dipping your pen into the inkwell to write could be messy and ink could suddenly blot and make a huge mark over the page. We were provided with blotting paper but still suffered blue fingers and sleeves, especially the left-handed kids who dragged their arm across the desk when writing. I was lucky to have my new fountain pen which was easy to fill from a bottle of Parker Quink at home. The ink claimed to be the best for all fountain pens and steel nibs. I can still remember its lovely faint aroma. Ballpoint pens, often referred to as 'biros' were being introduced, but not allowed in school as they were thought to detract from the development of good handwriting, which was so important back then.

We were going to be taught a variety of subjects: English, Maths, History, Geography, Biology, Art and Religious Education. Attitudes about what girls and boys should like were still very old-fashioned and we were divided up for some of our lessons. It was too bad for girls who liked football and boys who liked cooking. The girls were expected to enjoy sewing, cooking and domestic chores and we were even taught to iron clothes, supposedly to get us ready for marriage and motherhood. Boys would take technical skills and woodwork. That first day I missed my last school. I'd felt sad when I failed the 11-plus exam even though I'd worked hard and asked Jesus to help me pass. What more could I have done? I felt inferior being in a family group where some of my cousins went to grammar school. I will just have to make the most of it, I thought, buckle down and study hard. Hopefully things would improve when proper lessons started.

Relieved that the first day at big school was over we sat on the warm, crowded bus with all the older kids as we chugged back up the Twines on our way home.

CHAPTER 20

Teachers

The hot weather continued and during September an Indian summer set in which continued until mid-October. It gave us the chance to spend breaks and dinnertime in the playground and playing fields, having fun and forming new friendships. Respect for teachers continued and lessons were taught in a disciplined manner.

Unlike grammar schools, secondary moderns were generally deprived of both resources and good teachers. And we didn't learn Latin. Teaching back then was so different to today. It was all rote learning and the talk and chalk approach of primary school continued. Particular emphasis was put on learning grammar and spelling.

Of course, we could always read books and listen to the news on the radio or watch it on tele if you had one. But we didn't have access to real-time news updates that allow today's children to discover the happenings around the world. We didn't have the internet for online learning. Many of the kids weren't interested in doing anything academic in life or entering the professions or going to university, they were looking forward to leaving school at 15. Fortunately, we were taught practical subjects to a high standard. Secondary modern schools brought out the best in non-academic kids. And most, I remember, went on to do really well in catering, plumbing, landscape gardening and sewing. Many developed successful businesses of their own. Most parents in those days didn't tend to be stressed about their children's academic performance in school. Life in general was much less competitive.

Some mornings we all gathered in the main hall for assembly. It meant the school needed to make announcements about any changes that were happening or sometimes an outside person had come in to talk to us on different topics. It always seemed to go on for such a long time.

The mere mention of Miss Coe filled me with dread. She was a small lady with an angry face and a temper to match. She would rush down the corridor, her head bobbing from side to side, poker-straight hair flying all over the place. If she spied kids walking two abreast, she would glare at them and, hand held in a tight fist, forcefully thump the one walking on the inside in the back, shouting, "Single file only and hurry up" as she darted past. She seemed to enjoy intimidating kids. She was a tyrant and a bully. I remember having the misfortune of being in her needlework class. Marilynne and I were now in the same class with a friendly group of girls. Miss Coe became increasingly exasperated one day while trying to explain the difference between the "warp and weft". Taking a short intake of breath she grabbed a piece of flowery material and held it up saying, "This is the warp and as you can see it is very firm and has no give, or stretch." She pulled the fabric lengthwise. Then turning the fabric crosswise, she continued, "And this is the weft, it is less strong and it has some stretch." It can't have had much stretch as suddenly there was an almighty ripping sound as she tore the material. Silence. We all looked at each other in disbelief before the laughter started. Miss Coe was furious and we got a good telling off. I have never forgotten the difference between the warp and weft!

Janet Wright was bright and vivacious with a mischievous streak and she decided to play a practical joke on Miss Coe. We arrived in class early, Janet produced some plastic dog poo from her bag and placed it under Miss Coe's desk. "Let's see how long it takes her to notice it," she said with a grin on her face. Miss Coe appeared impressed to find us all sitting quietly eager to get on with the lesson. She walked round the class checking our sewing and I was hoping she wouldn't notice the dog poo. But she suddenly stopped and stood stock-still staring at her desk. We'd been rumbled. You could have heard a pin drop. She looked exasperated, the deep creases around her eyes exaggerated by her frown. She shouted, "Who has put that there?" No reply. Pointing to the lump of plastic poo she continued, "If the person who has put that there does not stand up, you will all be punished." She waited. The sound of chairs scraping against the floor broke the silence. We all stood up. We all got punished.

Mr Rain was our Religious Education teacher, a small, round man with a round face and round glasses, his dark hair thinning. He wore a dark-grey suit and walked slowly with a slouchy posture. He was an under-confident man with a nervous disposition, his lined face beset with worries. Mr Rain found it difficult to control disruptive students. It was usually one of the boys that started things by excessively talking, passing notes or giggling. Others would show off by asking questions with no relevance to the lesson. Soon everyone joined in until the noise got louder and louder and Mr Rain would be forced to interrupt the lesson in order to try and stop the chatter. The bad behaviour interfered with his ability to teach effectively and required large amounts of his time and attention. It was so unfair on Mr Rain and the students who wanted to learn. The stress, anxiety and worry certainly left its mark on him as he eventually went off sick. I remember Mum telling me that he had suffered a nervous breakdown caused by the bad behaviour of his students. I don't think he returned to the school.

I had enjoyed Maths at primary school but it suddenly became even more interesting when Mr Vanham became our teacher. The fact that he was a tall, charismatic young man with a calm persona might have helped! Mr Vanham was very approachable and passionate about his subject. He had respect from the class, even the disruptive ones behaved. He was a gifted teacher.

I shudder at the thought of PE lessons at secondary school. They were usually taken in the gym by Mrs Hartley, an overbearing teacher who enjoyed punishing her students – a good match for Miss Coe. I was an active child, but never good at climbing ropes, or wall-mounted bars, or jumping over the wooden horse. I could barely manage a forward roll. I would be in a very anxious state as we got changed, were ushered into the gym and formed an orderly queue. Following Mrs Hartley's instructions, we did each activity in turn. My biggest dread was the wooden horse; I was incapable of jumping on it, let alone jumping over it. I don't remember which teacher was taking the class on the day Janet Wright had a bad accident. We were using the beams and ropes to do forward rolls over the beam. There was suddenly a loud crack as Janet landed heavily on her bent arm. She lay on the hard floor in severe pain. There was no health and safety in those days and time seemed to stand still as we patiently waited for the teacher to come and help. Janet had fractured her arm.

We soon discovered that the punishment for forgetting your gym kit was to walk round the field. I remember purposely forgetting mine many times; I preferred the punishment to those dreaded lessons any day.

Miss Collins taught games. She was a short, curvy, well-toned lady with short brown hair and a healthy complexion. It was obvious by the way she ran round the hockey pitch that she kept herself fit. Miss Collins was strict but fair and I enjoyed being out in the fresh air playing hockey, netball and rounders. If she was unable to take our class, Miss Swift stood in. She was a petite, attractive lady and also had a pleasant personality. I never forgot my gym kit for games.

Sports Day was a big event each year. Students were picked to compete in events such as running, high jump, long jump and relay races. But I was quite happy spectating.

I found school showers a terrible experience as I was body shy back then and it sent me into a panic. We were self-conscious teenagers, all at different stages of puberty; either we were the only ones with breasts and periods or the only ones who hadn't got breasts and periods. Or we might feel skinny or fat, hairy or spotty. I shudder to think how we had to shower totally naked in a communal shower after PE with a teacher looking at us to make sure we cleaned ourselves. We tended to run through the shower avoiding the water jets if the teacher was out of sight. You could claim to be 'off showers' if you were having a period. But I seem to remember the teacher keeping a note of it. It was always a rush getting changed for the next lesson.

I vividly remember the sanitary belt, an elastic belt used to hold pads in place. It was pretty much the only option for young, newly menstruating girls at that time. Though tampons had existed since the 19th century and Tampax had been selling modern applicator tampons since 1936, the general view was that these were only for married women. Younger women were discouraged from using them because it was thought to be sexually improper which left us poor girls to wrangle with sanitary belts. The belt consisted of an elastic loop that went around your hips with small clips dangling at the front and the back. The pads had loops that hooked onto the clips. The pads were so bulky and uncomfortable; they rubbed your lady bits and it's a wonder we didn't all have bandy legs. I had a little zip-up bag to carry my pink belt and towels in. At least the belts came in different colours. It was a confusing time as we were so unbelievably innocent about it all. It was awful having to rush to the smelly loo and those incinerators to dispose of our used towels. You couldn't even use a wedge of loo paper in an emergency as it was as hard as greaseproof paper.

With the start of my periods came my migraine attacks. The first one started in a needlework class. It was a warm, sunny day and the classroom was very bright. I started to feel dizzy, sickly and sweaty, as my vision became very blurred and I was struggling to focus on the needle I was sewing with. I was frightened. Fortunately, it was the last lesson of the day and I just wanted to get home. The pain in my head was unbearable as I walked down the noisy corridor to catch the bus. I made it home just in time to be violently sick. Mum knew immediately what was wrong with me as she had suffered from migraine for many years. And she knew how to treat it. I soon found myself in bed with a cold, wet flannel soaked in vinegar over my forehead. The pain gradually settled and I started to feel much better. But it took ages for the chip shop smell to disappear.

I can still picture the class being marched to our first swimming lesson. We set off from school, walking to the main street in Bingley and then turning into Myrtle Place. Walking past the entrance to Myrtle Park, I longed to go in and play on the grass and watch the wildlife. But we were soon being ushered into the swimming baths. It was a cold, imposing Victorian building. Some of my class could already swim but I had never even been to a swimming pool before. The strong chlorine smell tickled my nose and my eyes felt dry and itchy as we entered the large oblong pool, the deep end at the top with its diving board. I watched the ripples of water glistening blue in the light. It was magical. We were soon split into groups, swimmers and non-swimmers. I was shaking with fear getting into the shallow end of the pool and only remember doing some exercises on that first lesson. But much worse was to come as we soon found ourselves forming a queue in preparation to jump into the deep end. The teacher held out a long pole with a metal ring at the end. In turn we had to jump in while clinging tightly onto the ring, relying on the teacher to pull us out of the water safely. It soon progressed to jumping in and going under the water with a rope around the middle. I was shivering, heart beating fast as I took a sharp intake of breath, pinched the end of my nose and jumped. I kept my eyes tightly closed as I plunged into the cold water. Then silence as I sank to the bottom of the pool. The rope felt as if it was holding me down and I started to panic and frantically move my limbs. I could feel myself drifting and gradually heard sound as I reached the surface. I opened my eyes and took a deep breath, relieved that I had survived the ordeal. I did learn to swim and still have my old swimming certificate from school.

The smallpox outbreak in 1962 sent everyone running to get vaccinated. The outbreak in Bradford came to light on January 11, 1962, after the death of a patient. And all the students were queuing up with their sleeves rolled up. After the vaccination we had to wait for a scab to form; the bigger it was the better – to be sure the vaccine was successful. We all had a sore arm and the injection mark scarred us for life. The smallpox vaccine, the first vaccine to be developed, was introduced by Edward Jenner, an English physician, in 1796. Smallpox is a debilitating and occasionally fatal disease that's highly contagious. It is no longer considered a threat, thanks to a worldwide immunisation effort that eradicated the disease by 1980. Smallpox is the only human disease to have been completely eliminated.

CHAPTER 21

Teenage Angst

I was no longer a child but a bona fide teenager. I can feel the excitement of becoming a teenager but my 13th birthday is a complete blur. I didn't enjoy having parties but guess our house would have been very busy that day with lots of comings and goings and my birthday would have been celebrated in a special way with lots of excitement, lovely food, fun and presents. I'd always enjoyed unwrapping presents and seeing what surprises lay inside. I can't recall any of my 13th birthday presents, but surprisingly can clearly remember an Easter Sunday when I was around five years old and Dad handing me a colourful box. I lifted out the Easter egg within, captivated by the beautiful white chocolate I held in my hands. I had never seen a white Easter egg before; it was glistening in the light and so delicate. How could I possibly eat it? I slowly returned it to the box and placed it on the bottom shelf of the cupboard in the parlour. Every few days I would lift it down to admire it. Months past but I still couldn't eat it. The egg eventually stopped glistening and went a mucky yellow colour. Reluctantly I had to throw it away.

I soon became a stroppy teenager, finding life both difficult and confusing. Mum said it was because I'd reached adolescence and was becoming an adult. But I was unsure where I belonged. Although I'd given up my childhood toys, stopped building dens and climbing trees, I still wanted to be active with my friends. I didn't want to spend as much time with my parents and other adults as I did when a little girl. I became rather withdrawn at home, wanting my privacy and spending more time in my bedroom. As I grew, so did my appetite. I started falling asleep later at night and had problems getting up in time for school. My self-esteem was low, trying to adjust to the changes my body was going through. My rapidly changing physical appearance often made me feel self-conscious, but at least I wasn't spotty. I found it difficult dealing with the emotional changes that accompany puberty, feeling uncertain, moody and sensitive at times. Peer relationships were a big issue and the opposite sex was becoming more interesting. I should have known it wasn't going to be easy, after all 13 is an unlucky number.

School life had changed a lot since being a newbie. Thank goodness I had managed to outgrow my pinafore dress and was now wearing a smart skirt for school. And I had outgrown my warm, fleecy liberty bodice with its squashy rubber buttons that took forever to fasten. Mum had placed great faith in its protective values against the cold. But I hated it, refusing to wear it at every opportunity. I wasn't enjoying school but had made some good friends in class. We often met up at weekends and during the school holidays. But it could be difficult keeping in touch as we, like a lot of families, didn't have a telephone at home. So I had to use the public telephone in the village.

The big red telephone box on the main street was easily recognised, you just hoped it was unoccupied and working. There was often a queue of impatient people waiting. You had to have the right coins, which wasn't too onerous because coins were in everyday use; no credit or debit cards in those days. The phone box felt cold with a strange, musty smell. There were compartments for telephone directories, but they often went missing, so it helped if you had the number to ring. After lifting the big black receiver, you put the money in the slot and dialled the number. Button A had to be pressed to be heard, or button B to get your money back if no one answered. As a child you didn't pass a phone box without pushing button B on the off-chance the last caller had forgotten to collect their leftover coins.

Having fun with friends was an important social outlet. I had increased independence from my parents and began to rely more on friendships. Marilynne and I spent some happy times together, going for long walks, going to the cinema, or just visiting each other for a chat. Marilynne's mum never failed to cheer me up; she was so friendly and full of life. I can still picture the summer's evening she was driving us home after a night out, all busy chattering. I was intrigued watching her pressing the pedals wearing very high-heeled shoes, as she drove up the steep Twines road out of Bingley. She must have been very clever to drive a car in those shoes.

My main mode of transport was my bike, which I could now manage to get on and off without a problem. It was complete freedom cycling around the village with the wind in my hair. I didn't see much of Andrea anymore as she went to the grammar school but I occasionally visited her in the school holidays. She had stopped selling white mice and always seemed to have her head in a book when I arrived. Her ambition was to become an English teacher. Her mum didn't go out to work and was often found at her potter's wheel, in deep concentration throwing clay on the wheel as it whizzed around. Andrea's world was so different to mine. We gradually drifted apart.

My family dynamics were changing. Helen had moved house; she was living on the outskirts of the village with Brian and their adopted baby girl. Denise was a lovely baby and I visited them as often as I could. Most of my cousins had left home and were busy working, but I occasionally had a sleepover at Cousin Marlene's. She still looked much older than me, wearing make-up and stylish clothes. But I felt quite grown-up, going to the cinema in Haworth with her, in my new cream court shoes with leather bows and one-inch heels. It seems strange that shoes were such a major part of my growing-up years!

My list of household chores was growing. I was able to wash the dishes at speed when I was meeting my friends; glasses and milk bottles first, then plates and cutlery, leaving pans with dried-on food until last. Jane was now seven years old and able to help with the drying, while Mum put everything back in the cupboard. I would soon be on my way out, putting the empty milk bottles on the step for the milkman to collect early the next morning.

It was a treat to have a fish supper on Friday night. Mum would rush home from her part-time job at the local mill, lay the table and put the plates in the oven to warm while I went for the fish and chips. "Don't dawdle," she would shout as I left the house, "we don't want cold chips. And call to see if Grandma wants anything bringing back." Grandma always fancied something bringing back. I don't know how she managed to eat with her two remaining front teeth, but she did. There were three fish shops to choose from. I went to Hillaries fish shop at the bottom of the village. It was always busy on Friday evenings with a long queue down the steps. The plates will be warm and kettle boiled and I will be in bother again for dawdling if they don't hurry up. I'd run up the street, quickly dropping Grandma's supper off and arriving home to be told it had taken me a long time. Thank goodness the chips weren't cold.

The job I dreaded was cleaning out the ashes before getting the coal fire ready to light. Thankfully Dad usually did it before going to work. It was a chilly job first thing in the morning. Taking the ash out isn't a fond memory, a gust of wind was all it took to get hair and face full of cinders. But the hot ash was put to good use in the garden, or on the front steps when it was snowy or icy.

Mum lovingly polished the upright piano that dominated our parlour and from an early age I looked forward to the piano tuner coming. I listened for him tapping on the front door with his stick and watched Mum helping him up the steps and over to the piano. I was fascinated by his long, nimble fingers dancing up and down the keyboard while he was in deep concentration, tuning the piano by ear. How did he know where the keys were when he was blind? It took him a long while to tune the piano and I kept very quiet and still, so he didn't know I was there. He always looked happy when he left. I was around 12 years old when Mum suggested that I learn to play the piano. I had already mastered the triangle, castanets and recorder and could read music so agreed to give it a go. One evening a week I walked to Mrs Cope's house on Parkside Terrace for my piano lesson. Mrs Cope was a gentle character with a lot of patience. She was a friendly lady with beautiful big green eyes, which appeared to light up when she smiled. She would often be playing the piano when I arrived, her big round glasses perched on the end of her nose. How I longed to be able to play like her. Doing endless scales up and down the piano was no fun and I didn't feel to be making progress, but Mrs Cope was very encouraging, and promised I would soon be playing proper music. Her son, Linton, was a couple of years older than me. He was a tall, lanky young lad with a pale face who always looked miserable, a grammar school boy destined for a better future. I couldn't understand why my mother was so interested in him. I'd no sooner return home from my lesson when the questions started, "Did you see Linton tonight?" she'd ask, "And what did he have to say?" Was she not interested in how my lesson had gone? It was years later that I realised she'd had her eye on Linton as a future son-in-law! I did eventually learn to play the piano and continued lessons up until leaving school.

CHAPTER 22

Fun of the Fair

It's hard to tell a remembered story in a straight line and the earliest memories can get confused and mixed together. But the funfair suddenly pops into my head. I must have been quite young when I started going to the fair as I can remember the reassuring, firm grip of my dad's hand. I had only ever seen light bulbs in white so was amazed by the bright lights in red, blue, green and yellow, the throngs of people and music playing. Stalls and toys were everywhere: teddy bears, balls, games, dolls on sticks, dolls in huge dresses – too many to count. There were lots of prizes to be won. The big wheel and rollercoaster looked like steel giants reaching for the sky. It was overwhelming; there was so much to take in.

But my teenage memories are much clearer. It was exciting when the fair came to Cullingworth. It didn't matter what the weather was like, even if it was raining we donned our raincoats and wellies ready to trudge around the wet, muddy field. Nothing would spoil our evening of fun. I'd arrange to meet my friends at the fairground gate so we didn't get lost in the crowds. It was noisy with excited people chatting, loud music playing, and the rumble of generators. The smell of burnt sugar candyfloss, burgers, chips and toffee apples mixed with diesel filled the air. The ride owners and stall owners were friendly – like one big happy family. It was time for carousel rides, trips on the big wheel, the chance to win a coconut or a toy. The fairground stalls were packed tightly together and were fresh, imaginative and full of fun. I'd have a go on the coconut shy, hook-a-duck, hoopla or darts, but would consider myself lucky if I managed to win a goldfish swimming around in a small plastic bag. I enjoyed going on the dodgems, but although the idea was to bump other cars, there would be signs reading, "This way round" and "No head-on bumping". Not that anyone took any notice; it was the thrill of bumping into each other that was the attraction. The waltzer was always busy as we scrambled to grab one of the tub-shaped cars. There was lots of screaming as the cars started to spin around, making us feel quite dizzy. But for extra excitement one of the young lads working on the waltzer would jump on the back of the car and spin it even faster. What an attraction for a group of giggling teenage girls! You felt unsteady getting off the ride, with lots of faces turning a sickly green colour.

My surge of teenage hormone levels appeared to trigger frequent migraine attacks. They often came on at the most inconvenient times, following trips to the fair, before school tests and exams, or before going out with friends. Mum didn't take me to see Dr Baird as migraine ran in her family. I was spending a lot of time in a darkened room with the cold, vinegar flannel on my head. I often wondered if the cold flannel would have worked without the vinegar. Had Mum picked up the idea from *Jack and Jill*? After all, Jack did go to bed to mend his head with vinegar and brown paper. Thank goodness she didn't use brown paper on me.

Many families were finding difficulty adapting to the National Health Service, which was established on July 5, 1948, several months after my birth, by its founding father and chief architect Aneurin Bevan, the Minister of Health. It was to be free at the point of use and available to everyone who needed it. Before the NHS, only the privileged few could afford health care. Mum dealt with all minor ailments – no rushing to the doctor with a cold or sore throat. I remember her mixing butter, sugar and lemon juice in an egg cup. I would eat it with a spoon to ease my throat and stop me coughing. I'm not sure it worked but it didn't taste too bad. Most injuries were soaked in salt water. A plaster was stuck on a cut or graze. Butter was rubbed on a bumped forehead to stop it swelling. It didn't matter what was wrong with us, Grandma would pop in with a bottle of Lucozade and it always did the trick.

CHAPTER 23

The Big Freeze

I remember bitterly-cold and snowy winters as I was growing up. I'd step outside, wrapped up warmly in my thick woollen coat, hat and gloves, thick socks and wellies on my feet. I'd breathe in the sharp, cold, crisp air of winter, feeling my cheeks and nose reddening. But I didn't care as I watched the snowflakes drifting through the air, covering the ground with a soft white blanket. I'd often meet my friends and we'd spend ages outside, rolling in the snow, throwing snowballs, sledging, building snowmen. We'd go home with red faces, blue lips and runny noses. I'd enjoy the heat as I removed my coat and peeled the wet, cold socks from my frozen feet. It felt so relaxing having a warm drink by the fire.

But the winter of 1963 was another story: The Big Freeze, as it was known, was one of the coldest winters on record in the United Kingdom. It began abruptly just before Christmas in 1962. The weeks before had been stormy, but then on December 22 it became bitterly-cold and windy. Blizzards followed, causing snowdrifts. Roads and railways were blocked, telephone lines brought down and some villages were cut off for several days. Farmers couldn't get to their livestock and many animals starved to death. The snow set the scene for the next two months as much of England remained covered until early March. I recall my bedroom being freezing cold and strangely quiet as I slipped out of bed and looked out of the window to see that everything was white. I hurried to get dressed and set off to school, hoping it might be closed for the day. How I would love to have a snow day. Walking down the street, the crunch of snow under my feet, I imagined getting warmly dressed and running out to join my friends, enjoying the magical scenery around me. The thrill and excitement rushed through my spine, I longed to be a little kid again, rolling about in the snow and having fun. But the bus was ready waiting and the day was spent in lessons longingly looking out of the window. I never remember our school closing, whatever the weather.

The winter didn't fully relax its grip until early March. Finally, the coldest winter for more than 200 years in England and Wales had ended and life returned to normal.

It brought back vivid memories of the winter of 1947 for Mum. She often spoke of the severity of the post-war winter and the severe flooding when the thaw came. She remembered the impact it had on communities, the freezing cold, the blizzards and the thousands of people who were cut off by snowdrifts. Life must have been difficult struggling with power cuts, frozen pipes, no TV or baths and children sent to bed hungry because there wasn't enough food – ration coupons still had to be presented for everything from eggs to pieces of meat, from petrol to bed linen. It must have seemed more unjust than during the war. Had 1947 weather happened today, it would be so different. There would be cameras, snow ploughs, deliveries, supermarket food and Facebook and Twitter teetering on overload.

The Big Freeze would be remembered most for its coldness, and less for its snowfall. The winter of 1947 was the opposite, remembered for its snow, less its coldness. But both winters were very cold and very snowy and hazardous to life. And for once, snow wasn't just for fun and games.

CHAPTER 24

Woolworths Girl

My first holiday without my parents was a school trip to Bavaria. I can see myself now rushing home from school, the words tumbling out as I excitedly described the trip and the places we'd be visiting. My parents were happy for me to go, but could only manage to cover the cost of the trip. I'd also need a new pair of hiking boots and spending money. I desperately wanted to go. Most of my friends were hoping to and it would be such an adventure. So, there was only one thing for it, I had to find a Saturday job. I soon found myself doing a Maths test at the Woolworths store in Bingley with two of my friends. Susan Oughton and I were offered a job. We were so upset Susan Ingham wouldn't be joining us. Susan Oughton had become a very close friend. She was a pretty girl with delicate facial features, her soft, clear complexion radiating health and happiness. She was shy and would easily blush, her round face going bright red. It became a source of embarrassment and the more she thought about it, the redder she became. She was soon nicknamed "Cherry" in the class. Susan was very artistic, her paintings and drawings were incredible. We spent time out of school together and I enjoyed visiting her family and having Sunday tea at her house. The table was full of irresistible food; we ate so much we could barely move. I often wondered how her mum stayed so thin.

Smartly dressed and very nervous I jumped on the early bus to Bingley for my first day at work. I wanted to arrive in plenty of time to give a good impression. Woolworths was represented in nearly every British high street then with over a thousand shops in the 1960s. Its 'personal service' trading model made it a huge employer, with a workforce of 100,000 people including over 50,000 working full time supplemented by part-timers and an army of Saturday girls and boys. In those days a typical sales assistant was paid £6 for a 40-hour week. Many joined at 15, which was the school leaving age. I remember being paid 15 shillings and nine pence for working on a Saturday; I always gave Jane the nine pence.

Work started at 8.30am and the store opened at 9am. We were greeted by the intense staring brown eyes of Mr Potts, the Store Manager. He was a slightly built man, black hair tamed with plenty of Brylcreem, furrowed brow and stern expression. Suddenly my mind went blank and my stomach fluttered. I was petrified. Did I really want to work here? Thank goodness Susan was with me. We were given a tour around the store before being taken to our counter. Susan was on the sweets counter and I was on the electrical counter, surrounded by light fittings, bulbs and lampshades. I would much rather have been on the sweets counter, as I knew far more about sweets than electrical equipment. How was I going to cope? I didn't know one bulb from the other.

Miss Jones, a pleasant young lady wearing lots of mascara and bright red lipstick, was to show me the ropes. The personal service model was labour intensive as there was very little automation. The store did everything by hand. The tills looked much like an *Open All Hours* till and they didn't add up the value of the shopping. Instead, you had to work it out in your head. No wonder you had to pass a Maths test to get a job. Miss Jones gave me a pen and paper in case I needed to write anything down. She showed me how to test each light bulb before selling it and explained how important it was to keep the counter fully stocked up. There was so much to take in and I would soon be serving customers by myself. It was soon time for Susan and me to catch up over lunch. A free cooked dinner and pudding were provided in the dining room, cooked on site. Mrs Bailey was a curvy lady with short, tightly permed hair and a friendly face with deep laughter lines. She was an excellent cook who always looked after us and would give us seconds as she thought growing girls who were working needed plenty of food to keep their strength up.

Serving customers started that afternoon with Miss Jones closely watching me. I had to be polite and smile at the customers. Everyone paid with cash as debit and credit cards weren't around. We had "old money" back then, the currency used in the UK until February 15, 1971, when Britain switched to the decimal system. There were three units of currency, the penny, the shilling and the pound. There were 12 pence in a shilling and 20 shillings in a pound, making 240 pence in a pound. There were so many old money coins: the farthing, halfpenny, penny, threepence, sixpence, one shilling, two shillings, half-crown (2s 6p). Banknotes were £1, £5 and £10. You would expect our purses to be bulging with all the coins, but things didn't cost as much as they do today, so you didn't need much money when out shopping.

Uncle Albert complicated things further: not only did we have to understand his broad Yorkshire dialect, but he used slang terms for the coins. A bob was a shilling, a tanner was a sixpence and a quid was one pound.

A few weeks after starting at Woolworths we were left to get on with it, serving customers on our own and making sure our counter was well stocked up. Every evening we had to go downstairs to the huge, dark storeroom. It was overwhelming with stuff piled up everywhere. Even the storeroom boy had problems finding things.

Before being dismissed at the end of the day, Mr Potts would come round with the supervisor to check our counters and empty the tills, checking the money was correct. It took ages; no wonder I sometimes missed the bus home.

I was managing well and enjoying the job when one day I was confronted by a tall, rotund man with puffy eyes and a mean mouth. I had politely served him, placing the banknote in the till and handing him his change. "I gave you a £10 note," he said, "and you've only given me change for £5." I was sure it was a £5 note he'd given me but it was in the closed till and how would I prove it? He became very angry, shouting, his face going bright red. The growing queue of customers had to wait patiently while a livid Mr Potts checked the till. The man left with his tail between his legs after being told it was a £5 note after all and I had given him the correct change. Lesson learnt: don't put a banknote in the till until you have given the change and the customer has checked it.

It was months later that Susan had a bad accident at work. The end of a busy Saturday, we hurriedly got changed for our evening out together. Most of the staff had left by the time we were heading down the stairs. We were busy chatting when she suddenly lost her balance. I could hear the thudding of her body hitting the stairs, her limbs tumbling over one another as she rolled to the bottom, landing heavily with a loud thump. I froze at the sight of her lying motionless with limbs twisted. Mr Potts was soon alerted and was not pleased. Susan gradually came round; she was battered and bruised with severe pain in her hand, but Mr Potts showed little sympathy. He was more concerned that he was going to be late home as he was taking his wife out for dinner. He quickly telephoned his wife and Susan's parents, before bundling us into the backseat of his car and taking us to the hospital. My memory now becomes slightly blurred as I vaguely recall Susan's parents soon arriving and Mr Potts having a brief word with them before rushing off. It was a long wait at the hospital and I had no way of contacting my parents as we didn't have a home telephone. Susan was very shaken by the fall and had severe tendon damage in her fingers. Her hand took a long time to heal following surgery and she was left with a terrible scar.

I remember the pleasure of my first paid job. Getting a wage packet with actual money in it gave me such a sense of achievement. My income increased when I started working during school holidays as well. Money was always tight, and I learnt to respect it. I had been told "Money doesn't grow on trees" often enough. I had learned to manage my finances from my parents and I'm so thankful. I soon managed to save the extra money for my trip to Bavaria, with some to spare. Working at Woolworths was good experience and taught me many life skills.

CHAPTER 25

Bavaria

It was a fine summer's evening as a group of teenagers gathered outside Bingley train station to start their long journey to Bavaria. I'd been getting ready for weeks and with my new hiking boots comfortably broken in and my bag packed full, I was ready to go. It felt quite emotional saying our farewells as Mum and Dad dropped me at the station. It was the first time I'd been away without them and I was going abroad for the first time. We now had a family car, a light-grey A35, so could at last travel in style. Mr Vanham, Miss Collins and Mrs Barron were already at the station organising everyone.

There was a steady stream of students arriving and it wasn't long before I spotted friends from our group. I remember the noise in the busy station with quick-paced footsteps, and the smell of grease, mould and cleaning chemicals filling the air. The train was already waiting, casting a shadow over the platform. It was a bit of a scramble as we were ushered along the narrow corridor, all wanting to share a compartment with our friends. The compartments had three comfortable seats on each side with fold-up armrests. All suitably seated, the stationmaster checked all doors were securely closed, blew his whistle and then the train chugged slowly out of the station. We were on our way. The train had lavatories at the end of the carriage; they were a bit smelly and to be avoided if possible. There was a notice saying they were not to be used while the train was stationary. Each compartment had a large window which could be lowered by heaving an enormous leather strap to release it. It didn't take long before the boys were getting told off for opening the windows and sticking their heads out. I'm unable to recall details of the journey but do remember feeling very tired as night fell. There were sleeping bodies around me, on the seats and curled up on the floor. But even the rhythmic sound of the train was unable to lull me to sleep. I just longed to be at home tucked up in my comfy bed. I joined some of the other non-sleepers in the corridor. The journey went on and on as I paced up and down. I was feeling sickly and shivery, desperate for sleep. It was a long night.

There is now a gap in my memory, as the next thing that springs to mind is feeling emotional with tears in my eyes. It is daylight and the rolling hills outside have been replaced by huge snow-capped mountains hidden by clouds. I had never seen anything so beautiful. It was surreal; I felt I must be dreaming.

My tiredness had left me by the time we reached the Sporthotel Konigssee. The dormitories slept four people; they were big rooms with a balcony at the back of the hotel overlooking trees. Mr Vanham was in the room below us, so we had to be on our best behaviour. I was pleased that Susan Ingham was in my room. We were in fits of laughter as we looked so grubby after such a long journey and had aching, swollen ankles. Susan managed to have only one swollen ankle which looked rather strange. We quickly unpacked, got washed and changed into clean clothes ready to explore our new surroundings.

I was mesmerised by how beautiful Konigssee was, with its emerald-green lake nestled between several gorgeous Alpine mountains. There was so much to take in.

But John was uppermost in my mind. I was anxiously waiting for him to arrive. Boys were my preoccupation at the time and John Firth was my first proper boyfriend. He was backpacking with his friend Christopher Ferris and had arranged to meet us in Konigssee. John was kind, incredibly imaginative and independent, a real free spirit with a serious case of wanderlust. He wanted to see the world and often set off backpacking alone with very little money to see how far he could get. Exploring excited him and he was good at sussing out new people, ideas and places he came across. I was outside the hotel with a group of my friends when he arrived. I can still picture him standing there; he looked so handsome. I glanced around. Where was Chris? They had been split up on the journey. I was so worried about Chris, having visions of him being lost in a foreign country. We had no way of contacting him. John was unconcerned, he was sure Chris would find his way and Chris did arrive shortly afterwards. The journey must have taken its toll, as he didn't look well. Miss Collins was really cross with John for leaving him. We didn't see much of them. John easily got bored if he didn't have continual change in his life and they were soon off on their travels.

My new hiking boots got plenty of wear on the trip. We visited St Bartholomew's Church on the border of Lake Konigssee. I loved the beauty and charm of the place. The lovely red domed church is at the water's front, framed by tall snow mountains. The water was so clear, it was a magical experience with breathtaking views, just like a postcard. I could have happily stayed longer but we had to fit in a visit to the Ice Chapel. This involved a fun hike and I definitely needed my sturdy boots. We were so disappointed when we eventually got there though as it looked like a dirty snow pile!

It was a lovely day when we walked along the riverbank to Berchtesgaden. It was a leisurely stroll through woodland and trees as we observed the scenery and wildlife along the way. I found Berchtesgaden quite charming and was fascinated by the Alpine-style buildings with their window boxes filled with colourful flowers.

I can remember visiting the salt mines in Berchtesgaden. We were given a black miner's jacket and hat to wear before climbing into an open train to take us deep underground through cold, dark, narrow passages. It must have been quite scary as I hate confined spaces. The train ride took around ten minutes before we arrived in an open area; it was so bright which seemed strange since we were underground. Then four of us at a time got on a slide, leaned back and slid downwards. At the bottom we looked at equipment involved in mining the salt. I also remember the boat ride across the underground salt lake with its special lighting effects.

Above Berchtesgaden is Eagle's Nest, the place high in the mountains where Hitler would stay. The hike there was enjoyable, listening to the birds and taking in the amazing views of the valley. But the bunker gave me a sense of evil. I found it difficult to comprehend that Hitler had spent time in such a beautiful place.

The holiday passed quickly. The teachers had made it interesting and fun. We met in a separate building in the evenings and had to dress for dinner in our school uniforms.

Bags reluctantly packed we were all ready for the dreaded journey home. It was late at night when a group of scruffy, bleary-eyed teenagers with aching feet strolled out of Bingley station. Dad and Uncle Clifford were patiently waiting for me. The family were on holiday in Scarborough but Dad wanted to make the round trip so I could join them for the second week. I was soon curled up on the back seat fast asleep with poor Dad driving back to the coast. The car quickly clocked up the mileage and was soon named "Dad's taxi". Scarborough somehow didn't have the same excitement after Bavaria. The trip had broadened my horizons and opened a whole new world.

John continued to be my friend and we spent lots of time together. He made me feel safe and was always helpful. I wasn't particularly good at English so he would occasionally help me with homework and in return I would help him with Maths. He couldn't resist climbing up to the clock tower in the last year at school with an audience of excited school kids cheering him on. It was amazing what he got away with. We went our separate ways after leaving school but two years later, when I had started my nurse training, we bumped into each other in Leeds City Station. Unfortunately, I was rushing to catch a train so only had time for a brief chat. The following year I learnt that he had been getting a gun out of the boot of his car outside a gamekeeper's lodge, when it accidentally went off and killed him. I never knew the full story but with his love of nature can imagine him happily working in an outside environment. I couldn't believe it. I was so upset. John's life was always rich, rewarding and full of surprises. He was only 20 when he died.

CHAPTER 26

Career Choice

At 16 I was caught up in the stress of GCE O-levels and getting ready to leave school. The lowest school leaving age at that time was 15, and some of the students had already left without any formal qualifications. The Certificate of Secondary Education (CSE) was introduced for students who were unlikely to achieve GCE O-levels so they had some sort of qualification. Unfortunately, it was too late for my contemporaries in 1964 as it wasn't introduced until the following year. There was plenty of work available back then, but society had certain ideas about gender roles and challenging those ideas became a major theme of the decade. As the 1960s progressed, men were not usually held back and were obtaining jobs like teaching and nursing that were traditionally held by women. But this was not the case for women wanting to become police officers or firefighters. Throughout the 1960s young boys and girls were given more freedom to pursue more diverse occupations. The most common jobs for women were secretarial work, shop assistant, hairdressing, nursing or teaching. Everything depended on the exams, as course work wasn't taken into account.

I was feeling anxious when Mum and I went to discuss my fate with the careers officer. We were directed to a brightly lit room by a large window to await our turn. For the previous five years I had got up, put my uniform on and gone to school. Now, the thought of leaving was a little terrifying and I'd be incredibly sad to be leaving my friends. Mum hadn't had many opportunities in her life. But she just got on with her role of housewife and continued to work in the mill without complaining. Mill work must have been hard as she often referred to it as the "Sweat Shop" and looked exhausted when she came home. Mum was supportive and wanted me to get an education so that I could make my own living and stand on my own two feet. I think she always wanted Jane and me to have the opportunities that she didn't.

We didn't have long to wait before the door flew open and a large man with greying hair, bushy eyebrows and a wrinkled face strode into the room and across to his desk in an ungainly manner. Mr Carter introduced himself and rubbed his hands across the smooth polished top before rifling through a pile of papers. My file was near the bottom. I looked at my list of job possibilities. Shop assistant was the first possibility, a job I'd be able to do after my experience working at Woolworths. A music shop would be interesting; after all I did play the piano. Or maybe a shoe shop, I knew quite a bit about shoes already. What about a secretary? I had already had some shorthand and typing lessons at school. Hairdresser might be another possibility. Teaching another suggested career, but I'd had enough of focussed studying. Time was ticking by and Mr Carter was getting exasperated.

The truth was I'd no idea what I wanted to do. Mr Carter shook his head at my suggestion of becoming a dental nurse and suggested I train to be a Registered Nurse. As I needed to be 18 to start proper nursing and refused to consider staying on at school, he proposed that I apply for the pre-nursing course at the Branch College of Institutional and Domestic Economy in Leeds. I would need to be quick as not many places were left. It was a two-year course where I would continue my general education plus subjects required for nursing. I would also be given an insight into practical nursing with a hospital placement for a day each week in the first year, and two days a week in the second year. And I would receive £16 a month. Mum was now sitting up straight with an expression of approval on her face.

I had never considered becoming a nurse and knew little about it. I was sociable, caring, liked helping people and, according to Mum, had been a very observant child. She reminded me of when I'd bought her a present of three glass dog ornaments. She had carefully placed them on the windowsill in the front room. One day I was playing in the street and Mum was busy polishing when she accidently broke one of the ornaments. It wasn't long before she noticed my face squashed up at the window, eyes glaring into the room at the two remaining dogs. So maybe I had what it took to be a nurse!

I reluctantly agreed to go for the interview; it would at least allow me to leave school. I was pleased to be accepted on the course along with a friend of mine, Pat Horton. An attractive, tall, slim girl with an open body posture, Pat had a relaxed attitude with a cool, calm presence. You never saw her being intimidated by anyone. She was very popular and a joy to be around. At school we were put in Mrs Barron's Biology class in preparation for what lay ahead. Marilynne had been accepted on the Demonstrators Cookery course at the college. The three of us were excited to be starting the next phase of our lives together.

How quickly the last few years of secondary school had gone. I think about my younger self when I was leaving primary school – a quiet, shy 11-year-old, full of innocence and fun. At 16 I could still be described as quiet in school, but had grown in confidence. We were all relieved when the exams were finished, but had to attend school until the end of term. The school leaving assembly seemed so final. My eyes welled up as we were saying our goodbyes. Marilynne was upset to be separating from her close friend Joyce Coltart. Joyce was a lovely girl with a wide smile, quietly spoken with an easy-going, kind and generous nature. I still have the same group of close friends today as I had then. Although change was inevitable, and new lifestyles and commitments had a habit of getting in the way, we have had happy times over the years, meeting up as often as possible.

CHAPTER 27

Sixties Culture

Cullingworth didn't change much in the 1960s and village life seemed to be still stuck in the austerity of the previous decade. The shops hadn't changed since I was a young child: Bert was still repairing shoes, Mr Passman was still the local butcher and Marilynne's parents still had the fruit and veg shop. The Friendly pub was just as noisy. Delivery vans still came up the street. Uncle Albert was still rushing about or drinking his pint pot full of strong Ringtons tea and Dr Baird continued to be a good attender.

Helen had moved to a bigger house in the village to accommodate her growing family. It had been a surprise when she had a healthy baby girl, Jane, in 1962 as she'd been told it was unlikely she would be able to have children of her own. Grandma Clark was now living in a ground-floor flat in Parkside Terrace. She coped well living alone and I often bumped into her shopping in the village. In the past I'd visited her on my way home from piano lessons, but while revising for exams I hadn't often had the chance to call. I had enjoyed walking down Parkside Terrace for many years, as I had to pass Mrs Grant's house, a friendly lady who kept a tortoise in her front yard. I would sit on the wall for ages, mesmerised as I watched the tortoise hide its head and legs under its thick, strong shell for protection. I'd wait patiently until its head and legs popped back out of the shell, and it started grazing around the yard and slowly climbing into a shallow-sided dish full of water to have a drink. I was usually late home after visiting Grandma Clark. Grandma Field now rented the small one-up, one-down house where Helen had lived at the top of Mill Street. It was common to rent your house back then and families tended to move frequently, either by choice or being asked to leave by the landlord. Grandma Field often popped in to see what we were all up to and would walk to the fish and chip shop, taking our order if needed. I was happy for her to do the fish and chip run. It didn't take long before she was rushing back up the street with the hot food. Mum never told her off for dawdling.

By the 1960s, the first teenage generation free from conscription emerged in Britain. Our parents had spent their youth fighting for their lives in the Second World War and wanted their own children to enjoy their youth and be able to have more fun and freedom. Suddenly there was this burst of creativity with new fashions, haircuts, cars and music, and for the first time the teenage years were being recognised as a special period between childhood and adulthood. We were already significantly different to those of a decade before. We were able to think for ourselves and have a say in how we dressed.

Fashion of the 1960s featured a number of diverse trends. Girls wore colourful cotton pedal pushers that ended mid-calf, with T-shirts or sleeveless blouses tucked into their pants, and blouses and dresses with rounded Peter Pan collars. I remember wearing a bright green knitted dress with no defined waist and a hemline just above the knee.

Mary Quant decided that young women needed their own style and hemlines got shorter and shorter. She popularised the miniskirt and shift dress, which became the epitome of 1960s' fashion. We were free to wear clothes that would have seemed outrageous ten years before. The miniskirts I wore often earned my parents' disapproval, some were so short you had to bend at the knees rather than bend over. And you had to have a pair of go-go boots to complete your outfit.

Supermodel Twiggy was a popular fashion icon of the era. She was stick thin and had big eyes with exaggerated eye make-up that gave her a unique look. She was one of the first celebrities brave enough to sport the pixie cut, solidifying the short haircut's position as a bold fashion statement. Jean Shrimpton was a famous model at the time and was known for her long legs, pouty lips and straight hair with bangs. Men's fashion also changed and teenage boys wore styles similar to what modern-day teens wear, jeans, T-shirts, sweatshirts and button-down shirts. The most iconic men's hairstyle, the mop-top, was popularised by the Beatles. The haircut sported a fringe of long bangs that grazed the eyebrows in front and was long enough to touch the shirt collar at the back.

It was the age of the mods and rockers, two conflicting British youth subcultures. The mod subculture was centred on fashion and music and many rode scooters, wore suits and other clean-cut outfits and listened to rhythm and blues, soul and beat music. In contrast, the rockers subculture was centred on motorcycling, and they wore leather jackets and motorcycle boots. Media coverage of mods and rockers fighting in 1964 sparked a moral panic about British youth and the two groups became widely perceived as violent, unruly troublemakers. One of the biggest defining aspects of the Swinging Sixties was music. Although rock and roll became popular in the 1950s, it wasn't until the early sixties and the emergence of groups like the Beatles, that music began its revolutionary changes.

Technological advancements drastically changed how people spent their leisure time. The early 1960s were a time when television evolved from the 1950s into a whole way of life, probably the biggest leisure activity for all ages.

My mind suddenly goes back to the 1950s as I fleetingly remember what must have been the first adult programme I ever watched. I recall it raining as I arrived with Mum to a house full of people huddled round a small television screen. I can picture the Queen with a large crown on her head and lots of pretty ladies in sparkly dresses. The Queen got into a gold carriage and grey horses were pulling it. I realise now that it must have been the Queen's Coronation on June 2, 1953, when I was five years old.

I was too busy to watch much television in my teenage years, but it was something we could do as a family. Western films were very popular which pleased Dad. I wasn't too keen but would join him if he was watching the series *Rawhide*. Clint Eastwood has been a favourite of mine since watching him playing the character Rowdy Yates, who was right in the middle of the action. But I never missed an episode of *Dr Kildare*. No wonder Richard Chamberlain became a teen idol in the title role.

Feminism began to become an influential ideology as jobs available to young women widened, allowing them to move away from home and become more independent. The biggest thing that would change women's lives was the contraceptive pill, which first became available in 1961 and was legalised for all women in 1967, giving them the opportunity to broaden their hopes far beyond marriage and motherhood. Other significant advances in this decade included the legislation of abortion in 1967.

CHAPTER 28

Dancing at the Mecca

Although I am grateful for the vast improvements in technology that have occurred over the years, I miss some of the simpler things that got left behind, such as simply just talking to each other. One huge difference between today's teenager and one in the 1960s is method of communication. We talked to our friends, by phone if we lucky enough to have one in the house, but mainly in person. No texting, e-mail, Twitter or Facebook. And what better way to encourage camaraderie and connection than going dancing.

For as long as I can remember, I have loved to dance, and feel lucky to have had my formative music years in the 1960s. My memories from then are far clearer than those from later years. I even enjoyed the dance lessons in secondary school, the barn dances, the Gay Gordons and the waltz, to name a few. In the discos we danced the twist, Mashed Potato, and the Locomotion. My passion for dance was intensified by Motown music.

It was very exciting getting ready to go to the Mecca nightclub in Bradford. Opening as a ballroom in 1961, the Mecca became one of the North's hottest nightspots, with artists queuing up to perform on its revolving stage. It was the place to be in the sixties. So Friday or Saturday late afternoon often found me getting my dancing shoes ready. Following a long soak in the bath, I started to prepare for the evening. Youth-led fashion was inspired by music and influenced the style and amount of make-up worn by the masses. It was all about the eyes in the sixties, and more dramatic eyeshadow and colours took off. The rest of the face was kept more natural and understated with pastel or pale lipstick. I wasn't allowed to wear much make-up so it was quickly applied. My look was completed with short, bobbed hair back-combed and stiffly lacquered, a colourful short dress with matching pantyhose, kitten-heeled shoes, plus a squirt of Mum's perfume. The pantyhose tights were a must for short skirts; we didn't want to show stocking tops.

I soon joined my friends at the Mecca in a long queue of people, all dressed to impress. Most of the girls were heavily made-up with false eyelashes and lashings of mascara. We couldn't wait to reach the large entrance of the long, single-storey building. The Mecca wasn't the classiest place in town but it had a vast dance floor, overlooked by a balcony that seemed glamorous, the ceiling covered with lights giving the impression of a starlit sky at night. The place was alive with loud music and groups of young people dancing, chatting and drinking. We were never asked our age but knew not to drink alcohol. The majority of dances didn't include a dance partner, so you didn't have to avoid dancing on your partner's toes. But most of the dances were unrecognisable, all you needed to do was move your feet and body around while singing along to the sound of groups like the Beatles, the Rolling Stones and the Animals. And enjoy yourself. Hours later, with blistered feet, I was rushing to catch the last bus home.

CHAPTER 29

Staying with Grandma

It was near the end of the summer holiday before I started college that Grandma Field's health began to decline. I arrived home early one evening to find Mum and Grandma sitting quietly in the kitchen. The only sound to be heard was the ticking clock. Dad and Jane were out. Kelpie our Yorkshire terrier and Tibby our black tabby cat were both curled up fast asleep, which was rather strange as Kelpie liked to run around yapping and he would routinely chase Tibby out of the house at night. Tibby was such a placid cat; she once sat quietly watching a mouse run across the kitchen floor, making no attempt to catch it. Mum told me that Grandma had had a "funny do". I wasn't sure what that meant but Grandma wasn't her usual self, and looked very pale, so I gathered she wasn't feeling well. I don't remember if she went to see Dr Baird but we had to keep a close eye on her to make sure she was managing to cope. Mum and Auntie Linda helped with her washing, shopping and cleaning. Every day my mother would plate her some dinner and I would deliver it to make sure she had a hot meal. Unfortunately, the Friday fish and chip run was down to me again.

I started to have the occasional sleepover at Grandma's house which was quite an experience. I would follow her as she climbed the dark, narrow stone staircase to the bedroom. It took a while to get to the top, as she kept stopping to catch her breath, and shaking her head saying "Hey lass, it's nowt getting old. You're a trouble to yourself and everybody else." But Grandma was never a trouble to me. I remember having to share Grandma's double bed. It was a large dark-wooden bed with a deep mattress and a couple of chamber pots underneath to save a trip to the privy at night. My chamber pot was the smaller one, a china pot with a handle, decorated with a pretty design. I never slept well at Grandma's as she had lots of heavy blankets on the bed and she snored. I'd make breakfast before going home. Grandma had a small pantry where she'd store everyday food items such as bread, butter, cheese and milk. Tins and packet foods were stored on shelves. Her only means of cooking was on an electric double-hob hotplate cooker. I'd make a pot of tea and we'd have cereal, often Shredded Wheat, fruit or porridge followed by toast or bread, topped with lashings of butter and jam or marmalade. Grandma liked her porridge made with milk which tasted much better than when Dad made it, the traditional Scottish way cooked in a heavy saucepan with water and a little salt. I could never understand why Grandma wouldn't eat eggs. She said the mere thought of them put her off. But she did enjoy a plate full of tripe with lots of vinegar.

Mum was so pleased that I would soon be starting college and it didn't take long for it to be common knowledge in the village. I only hoped that I'd live up to her expectations. What if I didn't enjoy college? What if I couldn't stick at it? I'd dressed up in my nurse's uniform as a little girl and made my dollies better, but it had never been a burning desire to be a proper nurse when I grew up. Grandma Field wasn't happy about my chosen career and begged Mum not to let me go into nursing. As a young woman, she had worked as a cleaner at Seacroft Children's Hospital and seen how hard the nurses had to work. She wanted an easier life for me. It was impossible to convince her that nursing had moved on since then and the conditions had improved.

CHAPTER 30

First Day at College

Iwoke before dawn on my first day at college, following a restless night's sleep, trying to imagine what the day ahead had in store. Smartly dressed with my large bag, a dry mouth and butterflies in my tummy, I rushed down Mill Street to the bus stop. I was relieved when Marilynne's happy smiling face appeared round the corner. It felt like the first day of senior school but we wouldn't be travelling on the school bus with lots of rowdy kids any more. It was a bus full of quiet adults commuting to work. I felt so grown-up. The bus arrived in Bingley with plenty of time to catch the Leeds train. Pat was anxiously waiting on the busy platform when we arrived. The train was on time and we were soon in Leeds running to catch the the bus to Holbeck. It seemed such a long commute, and after travelling on two buses and a train we felt tired already. It was going to be a long day.

The bus dropped us off near Czar Street so it was only a short walk to college. The building was a hive of activity with students rushing around trying to find their classrooms. We parted company as Marilynne went to find her classroom and Pat and I were pointed in the direction of ours. We were greeted by Mrs MacAulay, a smartly dressed lady with a warm smile and friendly personality, before being placed in groups which were named after influential people in Medicine. Pat and I were in the Fleming Group, named after Alexander Fleming, the Scottish bacteriologist and Nobel Prize winner best known for his discovery of penicillin. Our first day was taken up with general information about the course. We would be covering a variety of subjects to include Anatomy and Physiology, Health, Science, Maths, English, History of Nursing and Art – not forgetting the essential needlework and cookery lessons to prepare us for married life!

We had plenty of time to get to know the group and Pat and I soon became friends with two of the girls. Margaret Parker, a gregarious girl who was always smiling and full of life, was attractive, tall and slim with impeccable posture. Lynette Waller was a lovely girl, quietly spoken with a friendly disposition. Her pretty face was framed by a neat blonde bob and thick fringe. Our different personalities blended well and we spent lots of time together. Diana Gittens was one of the students who had already set her sights high. She was immaculate in appearance with her long dark hair pulled back from her face and tied up neatly. Diana was always courteous but faintly aloof. She'd already studied Anatomy and Physiology and seemed very knowledgeable about nursing. Her intention was to become a Nurse Tutor. My intention was to just successfully complete the college course.

Starting college was like entering a new world full of opportunities. It was a light-bulb moment for me when I realised how enjoyable learning could be. The tutors were helpful and encouraging and made lessons interesting. I had been introduced to new subjects and was fascinated learning about the workings of the human body. Practical lessons were fun as we practised basic nursing skills like taking temperatures and bandaging. The cookery course also covered special diets for medical conditions and nutrition for sick patients. And the Maths lesson included how to work out doses of medication. By the end of the course we would be well prepared to cope with nursing.

It was such a coincidence that my first placement was at Seacroft Children's Hospital where Grandma Field had worked many years before. I felt apprehensive having to travel alone on the bus as I hadn't a clue where I was going. Pat was lucky to have her placement at Leeds General Infirmary with Margaret and Lynette. I breathed a sigh of relief when I reached the hospital, a sprawling, single-storey building with a curious layout.

The unusually large size of the hospital site, with ward blocks located well away from each other by long corridors is explained by the past use of treating patients with infectious conditions. Seacroft Hospital was completed in 1904 as an isolation hospital for people with diseases such as scarlet fever and smallpox. After the Second World War, medical advances lessened the need for so many infectious disease beds and the use of the hospital gradually changed.

Feeling anxious and lost, I decided to ask a passer-by for directions. "Go in the entrance at the front of the building and head towards the clock tower," said a friendly young lady pointing towards a large red-brick tower covered in ivy. I thanked her and set forth to try and find my ward. The wards were connected by a series of long corridors, which were only roofed; the sides were left open. Rushing down the corridor, I tried to imagine how cold and damp it would be in the winter with the rain and snow coming in. The nurses would need a cape in the bad weather. I felt my heart beating rapidly and the muscles in my chest tensing up. I was minutes away from walking onto my first ward. A dark corridor led to a large kitchen where Sister Holleran was munching on a biscuit as she waited for my arrival. She was a curvy lady with an amiable disposition, wearing a blue uniform, her belt fastened beneath her large bosom with a large silver buckle. "Good morning, I gather you must be Molly Clark," she said with a smile.

"Yes, Sister, I hope I'm not late. It seems to have taken me ages to find you."

"No, you've managed to arrive on time. The hospital is like a maze but you'll soon find your way around. Let me get you a drink then I'll show you where to get changed."

Once dressed in my bright yellow overall (pre-nursing students were referred to as "Canaries"), we walked into the main ward. It was huge, with a high ceiling and tall windows. Rows of small beds stretched down either side. A separate ward had rows of cots for young babies. I felt very nervous and self-conscious walking down the ward, but Sister Holleran was kind and tried to put me at ease. The nurses looked smart in their neatly pressed uniforms. I worked with Nurse Jones for the day. She was a second-year pupil nurse doing a two-year course to qualify as a State Enrolled Nurse. Nurse Jones had such a caring manner and was very gentle with the children. She let me help with some of the jobs and I watched as she fed and changed babies, gave medicines and injections. The ward ran very efficiently with Sister Holleran in charge and she seemed well respected by her staff. It was an enjoyable but exhausting day, with only one more hurdle to overcome – to find my way back home.

CHAPTER 31

Grandma's Funeral

Christmas was soon upon us. At home the parlour was brightly decorated, lights twinkled on the Christmas tree, presents were ready to open and music played on the wireless. Even Dad's brass crocodile nutcracker and large dish filled with nuts hadn't been forgotten. But the house somehow felt cold and gloomy. How could we be happy when Grandma Field had become so poorly? Mum and Auntie Linda had managed to look after her at home with the help of Dr Baird and the district nurse. But when her condition started to deteriorate, she no longer could stay on her own. Grandma panicked at the thought of going into hospital, so Mum decided to care for her at our house. As there wasn't room to accommodate us all, Jane and I went to stay with Auntie Linda who now lived in a bungalow on the other side of the village.

They were strange times as we flitted between home and Auntie Linda's. The whole family helped; Auntie Ada was around most of the time and Uncle Clifford, who now lived in Bingley, visited whenever he could. There was a surreal emptiness when visiting Grandma. The bedroom was eerily quiet, only the faint sound of the ticking clock on the mantelshelf could be heard. Grandma was sleeping, her slim frame outlined by the winter sun shining through the window. As time passed, and her appetite became poor, my mother became desperate to get some nutrition into her. Perhaps a soft-boiled egg would fit the bill. But Grandma had never eaten an egg because she never fancied one. It proved to be a bad idea as she struggled to eat a small amount before being violently sick. Grandma was withdrawing from the world, she didn't seem interested anymore and was talking less. I felt afraid as she became confused, empty eyes looking past me in a daze. Did she even know me?

Dr Baird continued to be a good attender as he visited most days. The district nurse would call to help wash Grandma and make her comfortable. It was all beginning to take its toll on Mum; she was exhausted and looked so pale and thin. I remember an evening after Christmas, when Grandma had been sleeping most of the day, groaning and gasping for breath. We were in the kitchen having tea when suddenly there was a loud thud. Dad ran upstairs to find Grandma had fallen on the floor. Had she tried to get out of bed? Was she starting to feel better? Dr Baird soon arrived and Grandma was comfortably tucked up in bed with no ill effects from her ordeal. Early one morning Uncle Albert told us there had been a change of plan; we had to stay at the bungalow and Auntie Ada would look after us. Why couldn't we pop home? We knew it must be serious. Grandma died peacefully on January 2, 1965. Mum and Dad were with her along with Auntie Linda and Uncle Clifford. Why hadn't I been told what was happening? I was surely old enough to understand at the age of 16. It was early evening when we were told Grandma had died.

It was a cold, miserable day when we gathered at St John's Church for Grandma's funeral. I had never been to the funeral of someone so close to me before and was unsure what to expect. I vaguely recall the church filling with people as we arrived to take our seats on the front wooden pew. The church felt so cold, the sound of people talking echoed around the large building with its vast angular ceiling. I felt afraid as I glanced at the coffin in front of me, unable to image my grandma lying inside it. What would life be like without her? I didn't get a chance to say goodbye or tell her how much I loved her and I'd never see her again. The Vicar stood proudly at the front of the church near the coffin and everywhere went quiet as the ceremony started. There was a lot of standing up and sitting down as we listened, prayed and sang hymns. People around me were crying and dabbing their watery eyes. As I watched the funeral in silence I bit my lip to contain my tears. Our family left the church first, followed by everyone else.

It seemed such a long journey following the hearse carrying Grandma's coffin to Bingley Cemetery. Close relatives gathered around the graveside as the pallbearers carefully lowered the coffin into the grave. Red, swollen eyes were all around. Dad put a protective arm around Mum as she hung her head with a downcast gaze. The Vicar then said a few words before flowers and earth were placed into the grave. Grandma had now been laid to rest with Grandad.

Locking myself in the bathroom that evening, I could no longer hold back the tears. I was uncontrollably sobbing as the tears streamed down my face. Jane and I missed her so much, she'd been such a large part of our lives and we would never forget her. Mum tried to console us by saying that Grandma had lived to a good age, had lived her three score years and ten, and was on borrowed time. She wouldn't want us to be sad now that she'd gone. I didn't fully understand what Mum was saying. I knew a score was 20 so three score plus ten must equal 70. But where did Grandma borrow the extra six years from? I soon learnt that three score and ten is a biblical expression giving the lifespan of a human being, and borrowed time from death is an unexpected extension of life.

Psalm 90:10

The days of our years are threescore years and ten; and if by any reason of strength they be fourscore years, yet is their strength labour and sorrow; for it is soon cut off, and we fly away.

Grandma might have had a long life but it, as for many of her generation, had been a hard one. She would be busy bringing up the children while Grandad was working long hours as a hewer, a miner who loosens rock and minerals in a mine.

From the 1920s the training of hewers was legally regulated as a result of union demands. The training must have been difficult, as between his apprenticeship as a sorter boy and the exam, the trainee hewer had at least two years of practical experience. The hewer exam comprised practical and theory elements. The hewer was held in particular esteem by the other miners in the Pit, even though he had no authority over them.

Every week Grandma would wait at the Pit, along with many other women, for her husband to appear with his wage packet. Grandma would take enough money to feed the family and pay bills. But she always made sure Grandad had some spending money! The latter part of his working life was spent as a spring maker's labourer.

Although Grandma's life was mainly spent in the home, she could always get a cleaning job if money got tight. It must have been exhausting for her working at the Guide Inn, an isolated pub located on the moors between Cullingworth and Keighley. She would walk up the long, steep road out of Cullingworth early in the morning, whatever the weather, and do several hours cleaning before the long walk back home. Following Grandma's death, Mum learnt that she had given birth to several baby boys before she herself was born. It explained why my mother was much younger than her siblings. The babies had only lived for a short while and Auntie Linda vaguely remembered the babies crying as Grandma carried them around on a cushion to try and comfort them. Grandma never spoke about it. Perhaps it was too painful. There was no support or counselling in those days.

CHAPTER 32

Sick Children

Losing Grandma was the hardest thing I had ever experienced and I struggled returning to college after the Christmas holidays. Our pre-nursing group were soon gathered in the classroom, waiting for Mrs MacAulay to take the register. Glancing round the room, I could see the group with happy, smiling faces, dressed in their light-blue, long-sleeved nylon overalls, ready to get on with the day. Why did we have to wear these dreadful overalls when we attended lessons? All students had to wear them; but each course had its own colour. Maybe it prevented us from getting lost.

I soon found myself staring out of the window, unable to concentrate. Feelings of anger, fearfulness, anxiety and guilt would suddenly appear from nowhere, and I was finding my intensity of emotions difficult to cope with. What was happening to me? I was confused and unable to find the words to express how I was feeling. Sometimes I wanted to be alone and other times I wanted to be near friends and family. I often dreamt about Grandma and sensed her presence; many times I imagined her purposefully rushing up Mill Street with our warm fish and chips. Friends and family were a source of comfort and support, and I gradually began to feel like my old self again.

Fleming Group had gelled well. We were from different walks of life but all had the same goal, to become qualified nurses. With the exception of Art and Physical Education, I continued to find all subjects interesting. I was amazed to receive a high mark for my artwork, and a comment from my PE teacher saying "This student has a very good sense of rhythm" in my end of term report. Mrs MacAulay had always dictated our Anatomy and Physiology lessons while we quickly scribbled the information down, but things were to change now that Mr Evans, a good-looking young man with a sense of humour, was taking over the class. It took a while to get used to his unique method of teaching. He believed his students missed information while busy making notes, so pens were put down while he delivered his lesson in a light-hearted way, ending with lively banter. It was a fun way of learning and amazing how much information we remembered.

I began to feel part of the team on the ward at Seacroft Children's Hospital. Sister Holleran, who was often to be found in the kitchen, always greeted me with a warm smile, and I helped the nurses with their routine work as well as doing lots of cleaning. I became friends with Barbara Peacock, a first-year pupil nurse who had recently started working on the ward. Barbara was living in the nurse's accommodation but commuted home to Keighley on her days off. Working with her made me want to be a nurse more than ever, she was such an easy-going character, always had a smile on her face. Although we lived near each other, changing circumstances make it difficult to keep in touch, but we did unexpectedly meet again several years later.

Listening to the ward report, most of which I didn't understand, made me realise how much there was to learn. How did the nurses remember it all? Some children on the ward were very poorly and needed lots of care. Suzanne was a dainty, enchanting little girl, with pale skin and large cornflour-blue eyes, her short blonde hair a mass of thick curls. I soon become very attached to her. She was one of three children on the ward suffering from cystic fibrosis, a genetic disorder that affects the cells that produce mucus, digestive fluids and sweat. It affects mostly the lungs, but also the pancreas, liver, kidneys and intestine. A sweat test is done to analyse salt levels, and blood is taken to confirm the diagnosis. The condition is usually diagnosed in early childhood and although there is no cure, treatment can improve a child's quality of life and extend their lifespan.

I was near to tears as I helped Nurse Jones with Suzanne's nursing care. Her sad eyes looked up at us, as she struggled to breathe. We gently washed her and tried to make her more comfortable. But the coughing and sweating continued, and she was suffering with chronic diarrhoea, her stools greasy and smelly. She was given antibiotics for her lung infection, medicines to keep her airways open and thin her mucus, extra vitamins and minerals, plus a digestive enzyme to prevent deficiencies and ensure healthy growth and weight gain. Suzanne was only seven years old. "Would you like to help Suzanne with her lunch?" asked Nurse Jones. "It is very important that she eats a varied diet, full of protein and calories. We need to get her weight up. Sit by the bed and don't rush her. It's important not to force her to eat, but encourage her and let her go at her own pace. And don't forget to smile and chat to her." I felt humbled watching

Suzanne slowly eating her food, and thought about my life as a healthy seven-year-old, happily playing out in the street with my friends. How unfair life could be.

Samantha, the physiotherapist, was a young lady, tall and slim with thick blonde hair neatly tied back in a bun. She looked very professional in her white tunic. "Hello, Nurse Clark. Sister Holleran says you're going to help me with Suzanne's physio today," she said with a smile. I hesitated before responding, it sounded strange being called Nurse Clark when I was used to being referred to as a Canary. Samantha was easy to get along with and such a good teacher. She explained how essential physiotherapy was in the treatment of cystic fibrosis and should begin as early as possible. As Suzanne was so unwell, Samantha had to carry out chest physiotherapy, which consisted of percussion (patting on the chest and/or back) and postural drainage. Samantha gently patted Suzanne's chest to loosen the mucus, making it easier for her to cough up. She then positioned her so her head was lower than her chest and her back was patted allowing mucus to drain better from the bottom of the lungs and unclog the airways. Suzanne looked tired after coughing lots of mucus up, but appeared to have enjoyed us spending time with her. She was breathing easier and looked more comfortable. As we left she gave us a smile, but there was a grave look of sadness peeking through her expression.

Hospitals were miserable places for children and they had to follow the strict ward routine. The nurses were busy doing their work and hadn't much spare time to spend with them. Parents were under no circumstances allowed to visit children outside visiting hours. However, when open wards began to be replaced by private and semi-private rooms, it became impossible for the hospital staff to keep an eye on all patients simultaneously and this allowed parents to pitch in and give their children the essential comfort they needed. By the 1980s parents had the ability to visit their sick children in hospital and care for them with unrestricted access.

These days children's wards are far more inviting and play therapy is an effective way to make being in hospital a little less overwhelming. The health play specialists have a kind and caring approach, often working with parents and carers as well as the children to reduce the stress and anxiety of hospitalisation.

CHAPTER 33

Learning to Drive

Motoring really took off in the 1960s. So at the age of 17, like most of my friends, I applied for a provisional driving licence. It wasn't that I had any burning desire to learn to drive, but it would be a new challenge and I wanted to prove to myself that I could do it. The first step was to contact Ronnie Noon, a driving instructor who had come highly recommended, having a high pass rate. First lesson booked, I skimmed through the Highway Code, and spent time in Dad's car familiarising myself with the pedals and gears in preparation for the ordeal.

I'd had an early night to bed but was unable to sleep, nervously thinking about what lay ahead and hoping Ronnie had lots of patience. Why was I doing this? It suddenly seemed pointless; I wouldn't be able to afford a car for many years. A bright spring morning found me bleary-eyed, standing outside Passman's Butchers, suitably dressed in comfortable clothes and flat shoes, anxiously waiting to start my first lesson. A pale green Ford Cortina with a white roof and displaying L-plates soon arrived and parked up in front of the War Memorial on the opposite side of the road. Ronnie was a large man with dark hair, a neatly trimmed moustache and a booming voice, and introduced himself with a wide smile.

As the main street in the village was very quiet in those days, it was ideal for my first lesson. Ronnie looked at my provisional licence and checked my eyesight by asking me to read the number plate of a parked car before teaching the fundamentals of the car controls. Was I expected to remember what all the buttons, levers and pedals were for? Minutes later found me in the driver's seat ready to go through the safety check – known as the 'cockpit drill'. I was so petite, I could barely reach the pedals. It wasn't a problem for Ronnie as he pushed the seat forward, and then gave me a large cushion to sit on so I had a clear view of the road. He explained about checking doors and mirrors, moving off and stopping; my head was bursting with information. The theory was now completed and I still had an hour's lesson left. What now?

The big moment had arrived as I was instructed to get ready to pull away from the kerb when the road was clear. Surely he didn't expect me to drive on my first lesson, when I hadn't even had time to process all the information he'd thrown at me? I started the engine, pressed and held the clutch down with my left foot and selected first gear. With a clenched jaw and tight grip on the steering wheel, I pressed the gas pedal and slowly brought the clutch up until finding biting point. After checking my surroundings, rechecking mirrors and indicating, I was ready to move off. As I released the handbrake, the car juddered and stopped. Ronnie sat quietly while I kept stalling the engine. I didn't seem to have enough arms and legs! At this rate we'd never get anywhere. I was frustrated and near to tears, when a plank of wood suddenly appeared and was pressed on my foot to teach clutch control. It worked. I could now find the biting point and move off smoothly. Pulling in was much less traumatic and we were soon tootling up the road on our way to Halifax. It was a tiring lesson as I drove there and back, with Ronnie making good use of his dual controls at junctions and roundabouts.

With a few lessons under my belt, Dad offered to take me out in the A35 for some practice. And did I struggle! It had a three-synchromesh gearbox and it proved to be difficult getting up steep hills in second gear. Changing down to first gear took a lot of effort and skill as you needed to double-clutch by pressing the clutch and lifting the accelerator while going into neutral, then back on the accelerator, then back on the clutch to put it into first gear. If you didn't do it correctly, you heard a loud grinding noise, and if you weren't quick enough, the car started rolling back down the hill. So it was a good idea to get your speed up when approaching a steep incline.

Being an old car, the A35 had trafficator indicators, operated by a dash switch that swung out a little lever-like arm. The system was not satisfactory because the mechanism tended to jam so that the arm was either stuck in or out all the time and if you turned the engine off before the trafficator had come in it would stay sticking out. I remember hitting the inside of the pillar to make it either rise or fall. No wonder we had to learn hand signals; it was such a palaver. The handbrake was on the opposite side to the one in the Cortina which added to the confusion. So my lessons with Dad were short-lived.

I had a brief break from driving lessons when I left home to start my nurse training. But Ronnie and his plank of wood worked wonders and I was soon ready to take my test. This was one of the most nerve-racking experiences not helped by the fact that the chief examiner was sitting on the back seat assessing the examiner. It was impossible to ignore him as I could see his face every time I looked in the rear-view mirror. The driving test fee was £1 in 1967. It included reading a number plate from a distance of 67 feet to check eyesight, and answering questions about the Highway Code during the practical test, which was replaced by the theory test in 1996. Demonstrating hand signals continued until 1975. Ronnie congratulated me on passing my driving test before telling me that it didn't mean I could drive, just that I was safe to drive. But it became clear what he meant as he drove me home; watching him drive made me realise that I needed a lot more practice. I didn't drive again until I bought my own car three years later.

CHAPTER 34

Gas Lights

September came round again and our second year at college started full-on. The work had become rather intensive, and then there was plenty of homework to do. In bad weather we often missed the bus connection home, so Marilynne and I would shelter in Bingley Library and start our homework there. I liked to get it out of the way so I could then relax and enjoy myself. But Pat had different ideas; she would often leave the weekend homework until the commute to college on Monday morning. How she concentrated on the noisy train, I will never know. She sometimes needed my help but always handed her completed homework in on time.

But it didn't stop us having a full social life. I enjoyed walking, playing tennis, riding my old bike, going dancing, going to the cinema and going out with boyfriends. I had little time left to watch television although we now had three channels to choose from. We had to wait until 1966 for programmes to be broadcast in colour. It was at the Mecca ballroom where Marilynne first met John, a likeable young man with a pleasant personality. He was tall and slim with neatly styled brown hair. They soon clicked. I was 'playing gooseberry' when John's friend Martin arrived to save me. Martin was in his final year at grammar school, a tall, lean young man with a wide smile and a sense of humour. Marilynne started dating John and I started dating Martin. Arriving home one Saturday afternoon I was surprised to find Mum in the kitchen, enjoying a cup of tea and cake with John. What was he doing here? How did he know where I lived? It soon became clear that John had travelled on the bus from Halifax to pay Marilynne a surprise visit, but as there was no one at home he decided to see if she was spending time with me. John was so disappointed. But Mum thought he was a charming young man and had thoroughly enjoyed his company.

I frequently went to the cinema in Keighley at weekends. The common meeting place was under the clock in the bus station. It was always busy with people constantly checking the time. Had their friends been delayed or, worse still, had they been stood-up? Martin was always on time. I often caught the last bus home at 11pm on Saturday nights. I would then run up the street, passing the drunks staggering home from the Friendly pub. Fortunately, electric street lamps had replaced the gas lamps and it was much brighter. Mum was relieved when I arrived home safely.

I remember the gas street lamps when I was a young girl as we often used the lamp posts as winning posts when playing in the street. The light was greenish, eerie and flickering. It's hard to imagine a time when a team of lamplighters lit the gas lights every evening, then put the lanterns out every morning. Shortly after the Second World War clockwork timers started being installed in street lamps, so they came on and went off automatically. But every so often a man with a ladder would visit to wind up the clockwork mechanism, service the lamps or repair the panes of glass that often got broken.

I was spending little time with my family, but if I managed to roll out of bed early I could snatch some quality time for a quick catch-up with Dad over breakfast. Dad was a quiet man, often deep in thought. He rarely spoke of his life before meeting Mum but he would tell me about his teenage years growing up in Scotland, and cycling with his friends. He had such fond memories cycling from Edinburgh to Portobello, then along the Promenade overlooking the beach filled with families swimming and sunbathing. It was after Dad's death before I first visited Portobello. It was a quiet, depressing area. The beach was empty and the Promenade had hardly any attractions specific to a seaside location. Dad would have been devastated to see how run-down it had become. We came across a wooden plaque describing the area before the start of the First World War. It displayed photographs that met Dad's description, a thriving seaside town full of happy visitors. I was pleased he had retained those memories as I looked out to sea with tears in my eyes. Hopefully the 21st century will see the emergence of community activities, transforming it to its former glory.

Dad didn't say much about his war experience either. I recall him telling me of a bomb hitting below decks when he was sailing to North Africa. He would never forget the screams of the cook as boiling fat spilled over him. Dad was one of the men who volunteered to go down to rescue wounded men and bring the dead back onto the deck. My sister Helen was a young girl living in Scotland with my mother and Grandma and Grandad Clark when she remembers a telegram being delivered saying Dad was missing. It must have been a dreadful time for the family as they anxiously waited for further news. He was later found wandering around shell-shocked. Dad must have returned home, like many soldiers, with invisible psychological wounds of war.

CHAPTER 35

ENT

The year was flying by as we continued cramming the work in. Why had we to learn all this stuff? It was a bitterly-cold morning as we set forth to the sewage works. The visit was thought to be ideally suited as a practical element for students studying a range of subjects which unfortunately included Science. Maybe it would help our understanding of the environment – but was it vital that we understood the process of sewage disposal to become a nurse? We traipsed around the plant, surrounded by water and sludge, the smell quite strong and overbearing. Mum insisted I wear my warm, long woollen coat on such a cold day. It was a bad idea as the smell clung to the woollen fibres and it was many weeks later, following lots of cleaning, that I was able to wear my coat again. No wonder we had difficulty eating our packed lunches. Even Margaret lost her appetite which was unheard of. I can imagine her on our weekly trip to the chippy sitting outside enjoying her large portions of fish and chips with lots of salt and vinegar. They always tasted better eaten outside in the fresh air. The rest of us were packed full but Margaret somehow managed to also chomp her way through a whole packet of fig biscuits! How did she keep so slim? She still finds it impossible to resist fig biscuits.

My second-year practical placement was at Leeds General Infirmary, conveniently based in the centre of Leeds and only a short walk from the train station. The longest-established of the City's hospitals, the infirmary dates back to October 1767 when it was set up "for the relief of the sick and hurt poor within this parish" in a private house in Kirkgate, close to where Leeds market is today, as a temporary measure. Its first purpose-built facility opened in 1771 and that small building began a process of almost continual expansion to try and keep pace with the growth of the township of Leeds during the Industrial Revolution.

Construction of the current hospital in Great George Street started in 1863 to the designs of Sir George Gilbert Scott. Before drawing up the plans Gilbert Scott and the Infirmary's Chief Physician, Dr Charles Chadwick, visited many of the great contemporary hospitals of Europe. They were particularly impressed by those based on the pavilion layout recommended by Florence Nightingale, and adopted this for the new Infirmary. It featured the latest innovations, with plenty of baths and lavatories throughout, and a system of hydraulic hoists to reduce the stress of lifting on nurses and attendants. The new hospital was officially opened on May 19, 1869, by Prince Albert, the Prince of Wales.

Gilbert Scott's Infimary remains one of the great Victorian icons of Leeds but over the years it has burst out of its original boundaries with the addition of a multitude of new wings in often wildly divergent architectural styles. I recall my first day at the Infirmary, arriving at Great George Street, relieved and out of breath. The building with its Victorian Gothic frontage in red brick looked very impressive and I stopped to admire the grand, decorative entrance before asking for directions. I felt so small hurrying along the corridor with its high ceilings and Venetian Gothic windows, in search of the Ear, Nose and Throat Department.

The hospital was so busy, porters pushing trolleys, doctors in their white coats and nurses in their smart uniforms rushing about. How I longed to be wearing a proper nurse's uniform instead of my Canary overall. The nurses looked so pretty in their below-knee dresses, white starched aprons and collars, thick belts, black stockings and smart shoes. But it was their fancy hats that most interested me. They were pinned neatly to the front of the hair and fell in a flap at the back; it was fascinating how the air wafted the flap gently behind them as they moved about. How was it possible to transform an oblong piece of starched material into such a fancy piece of headwear? The sides of the length of material were folded over to meet in the middle, then folded in half widthways using lots of pins to hold it together. It was so confusing. The word 'origami' springs to mind; it must have taken hours of practice to perfect the art.

The ENT Department was always busy treating conditions affecting hearing and balance, smell or taste, along with problems with swallowing and breathing and head and neck tumours. Hospital etiquette was very strict. You had to be respectful to anyone senior and refer to them by title and surname only. There was a hierarchy, but also a strong sense of being part of a team. A proportion of an ENT surgeon's time was spent in the outpatients clinic, managing conditions medically without the need for surgery. The examination room was quite alarming with trays set with shiny, barbaric-looking instruments – speculums to dilate orifices to see inside, tongue depressors, an array of forceps, to name a few. Lights and mirrors were everywhere with the doctor sitting proudly behind his desk wearing a head mirror. I was relieved not to be a patient. The nurses assisted in carrying out treatments. A large number of children were seen with tonsillitis, hearing problems and blocked noses. But why do kids enjoy shoving foreign bodies in their orifices? My previous experience working on the children's ward proved to be invaluable when helping to calm them down before toys, sweets, or whatever else they'd decided to stuff in their ear or up their nose, was retrieved. It took many trips to X-ray in search of foreign bodies they shouldn't have swallowed. Tonsillectomy was fashionable in the 1960s and regarded as a panacea for upper respiratory tract problems.

Ear syringing was a common practice. It's amazing what you can find in blocked ears apart from hard wax, all sorts of foreign bodies such as cotton wool balls and buds and matches. Some ears had been blocked for years and the smell was often putrid. Patients regularly had to have them syringed several times but, like everyone around them, were grateful when they could hear again.

Epistaxis is bleeding from the nose, caused by damage to the lining of the nasal cavity. Nosebleeds aren't usually a sign of anything serious. They're common in children and most can be treated at home. But the nosebleeds that need medical attention usually affect adults. It was a cold winter's morning when I entered the clinic to the frightening vision of Mr Potts sitting upright on the trolley holding a wad of tissues and a kidney dish with profuse bleeding from his nose. He was not an especially tall man but was large, with stocky limbs, a pot-belly, grey hair and a bushy beard. Had Santa Claus arrived early I wondered. He was complaining of feeling dizzy and sick, while struggling to breathe through his mouth. An ice pack had been applied to the bridge of his nose, but the blood continued to pour. His nose was quickly packed to stop the bleeding before he was rushed off to the ward for observation of his high blood pressure. The work in ENT was so interesting and gave me the opportunity to meet people from all walks of life. I looked forward to starting my proper nurse training.

CHAPTER 36

Interview at Huddersfield

"You need to start thinking about applying for your nurse training," Mrs MacAulay had informed us. I was only four months off my 18th birthday and was undecided where I wanted to train. Most of my friends were applying to Leeds General infirmary, but I had read about a new hospital being built in Huddersfield and quite fancied a change. Should I apply to Leeds with my friends or Huddersfield where I wouldn't know anyone? I pondered over it for ages. I'd never visited the town of Huddersfield before, but it wasn't too far from home and I could come home on my days off. I would learn to become more independent there and make new friends. It would be an adventure. The thought of working in a brand-new hospital eventually swayed it for me. So my application letter was written and I was soon called for an interview. I was up bright and early, and put on a smart white blouse and blue pleated skirt, eager to make a good impression. We set off in the winter sunshine on our journey to Huddersfield.

My interview was in the old Huddersfield Infirmary, situated in the industrial centre of town with its mill chimneys and soot-grimed buildings. Built in 1830 by Joseph Kay and opened in 1831 to designs by architect John Oates, the hospital had impressive original sandstone columns identical to those on the nearby Huddersfield railway station. Once the primary treatment centre for the West Yorkshire town, the building closed after 136 years of health care services in 1967 with the forming of the new Huddersfield Royal Infirmary.

Dad parked the car in the public car park in front of the old hospital, overlooked by a large statue of King Edward VII. The building looked very imposing with its large sash windows and grand entrance modelled on a Greek temple. I went up the stone steps and stood beneath an ornate lamp to compose myself before entering through the green double-doors where I was directed to Matron's office. The hospital was becoming increasingly unfit for purpose, with terrible overcrowding in the wards and nurses and doctors working in poor conditions. Unfortunately, I would have to work there until the new Huddersfield Royal Infirmary opened its doors. I could only imagine the new spacious, modern hospital with double the capacity of beds, and the very latest in surgical aids and techniques, five operating theatres, a maternity unit and visitor facilities together with a radio and phone for each patient.

I only have a vague recollection of my interview but remember being shown into a large room with a dark-wooden desk. Matron Cora Nicholson was sitting behind the desk wearing a blue uniform with a frilly hat perched on her head. She greeted me with a warm smile. "Good morning, Miss Clark, it's nice to meet you. Do take a seat." She said that a Miss Hickman, the senior tutor, would be joining us shortly and the thought of two people interviewing me was a bit daunting. There were some widespread nursing shortages at the time, forcing new tactics for recruitment and retention. Matron had recruited nurses from overseas due to shortage of applicants to staff the new hospital, so hopefully I was in with a chance.

I startled as the large wooden door creaked open and Miss Hickman breezed in. I guessed her to be in her mid-forties, a slim lady with short dark hair, dressed smartly in a fitted purple uniform with a starched white hat on her head. "Sorry I'm late, Matron, I got a tied up with one of the students," she said breathlessly. "That's fine; we were just having a general chat before you arrived. Can I introduce you to Miss Clark who is hoping to start her training with the next set of students in April?" Miss Hickman gave me a smile before taking her seat next to Matron. I now felt outnumbered and a little uneasy as Matron asked, "Why do you want to become a nurse, Miss Clark?"

The room went quiet as they both waited for my reply. I couldn't say I'd had no idea what I wanted to do when leaving school, and somehow just happened to find myself on the pre-nursing course! Remembering how I helped care for Grandma when she was ill, I cleared my throat and replied: "I enjoy caring for people when they are ill. I am finding the pre-nursing course very interesting and thoroughly enjoying my hospital placements. I know nurses have to work long, gruelling hours, but feel it will be an interesting and rewarding career."

I soon began to feel more relaxed and my interview passed quickly. Matron stressed how hard the work was, with long hours, different shift patterns plus night duty. The pay was low and we only had one day off each week. When were we expected to fit in all the studying? But she convinced me it was a worthwhile career. Miss Hickman had an air of authority about her; I could imagine her being an excellent but strict tutor. I didn't have to take the entrance exam as I had the educational qualifications required, and had recently gained a further GCE O-level in Human Biology. I was accepted into nurse training pending a satisfactory medical examination.

On the way home Dad did a detour to the suburb of Lindley, around three miles from Huddersfield town centre, to see the new hospital site. The sun was still shining and although the hospital looked far from completion, it was in bright surroundings and I was able to see green fields. I had a strong feeling I would be very happy working there.

It was sad leaving college and all my friends, but we would keep in touch and meet up from time to time. Those college years were amongst the best in my life, and I feel so lucky to have been there with such dedicated teachers. I was full of optimism and ready for the next chapter in my life.

CHAPTER 37

Student Nurse

My eyes welled with tears as I took one last look at my bedroom to check that I hadn't left anything behind. I was so attached to that small back bedroom with all its memories; the fun times playing as a young child, getting ready to go out dancing, listening to the Top Ten singles on Radio Luxemburg on Sunday evenings and the many visits by Dr Baird when I was poorly. My small brown solid suitcase with its shiny metal clasp was full of my clothes, books and toiletries. I closed the bedroom door behind me and lugged the suitcase down the stairs. It was a dark, gloomy, rainy day in January 1966. Jane had already left for school. Mum was trying to hurry me along and Dad was waiting patiently in his car outside the front door to take me to Huddersfield to start my general nurse training. I felt cold stepping out into the street dressed in my thin jumper, skirt and jacket. As usual I wasn't dressed appropriately for the winter weather. Mum looked a forlorn figure as she locked the door behind her and jumped into the car. Dad put my suitcase in the boot and we were soon on our journey. I felt anxious leaving the security of our small terraced house. The street was quiet at this time in the morning. A small group of mums were in deep conversation walking down the street after taking their kids to school but vans weren't out yet delivering their goods, the neighbours weren't cleaning windows and scrubbing steps, and the Friendly pub was closed.

We were on our way to Huddersfield to meet with Matron and discuss my welfare, as at that time the age of majority was 21, but nurses often started training at 18. So the hospital had almost legal guardianship over you throughout your training. As I was still only 17 I would have to work as a cadet nurse for a while before starting my nurse training. Mum was quietly sitting in the passenger seat and Dad was concentrating on his driving, he didn't want to be late. I could sense the sadness during the journey. I didn't appreciate that it was also going to be a big change in my parents' lives as well as mine. Mum said: "You'll be back before you know it, Molly. You're only two bus rides away and you can come home on your day off each week." The traffic was heavy and the 16-mile journey seemed to take so long. It was pouring with rain as Dad parked the car, with plenty of time to spare. The old hospital looked less inviting on such a grim day and we waited for the rain to ease off before Dad got my luggage from the boot.

Once in the hospital we took a seat outside Matron's office. We must have looked like the 'three wise monkeys' sitting quietly in a row. I was interested watching people passing, some were smiling and others had worried faces. Staff bustled along the corridor, doctors in white coats with stethoscopes hanging around their necks, porters chatting to patients as they wheeled them on trolleys and official-looking people dressed in smart suits. Where were they all going? "Are you waiting to see Matron?" asked a stern-looking Nursing Sister taking a seat beside me. "Yes, we have an appointment with her in five minutes," I replied. "Well, hopefully she won't take long because I have a busy ward to run," she retorted. I took an instant dislike to the lady who looked well passed retirement age, with wispy short grey hair stuck out beneath her white frilly hat tied under her chin. Hopefully I wouldn't have to work on her ward. Matron soon opened the door and beckoned to us. "Good morning, Miss Clark, do come in with your parents." There followed a short discussion and my parents were assured that I would be well looked after. I felt like a small child being adopted! Mum and Dad said their farewells and I was left waiting in the corridor for the Home Sister to take me to my room. My stress levels rose at the sight of Sister Kay waddling towards me, a small rotund lady with a miserable face and ungainly gait. She escorted me to my room in the nurses' home. Standing with her arms folded under her ample bosom, she informed me of the strict rules and regulations. I thought I was going to be a nurse not joining the army! I knew I had to get used to it as all student nurses had to live in until they were 20 unless married.

My room was very depressing, with high ceilings and bland walls. The window was so high I was unable to see the outside world. The bed, wardrobe and dressing table were in dark wood, the bare floorboards creaky with a threadbare rug at the side of the bed. In the corner of the room were a washbasin and mirror; bath and toilets were at the end of the corridor. Sister Kay instructed me to unpack and get dressed in my uniform and said she would return shortly to take me to the ward for my first shift. I hadn't realised that I would be expected to work on my first day. I was near to tears, missing my parents already and feeling very alone and apprehensive.

My cadet uniforms were neatly piled on top of my bed. I felt disappointed unfolding the first one which could only be described as resembling a sack, both in style and colour. It didn't improve with wearing, being far too wide and long to flatter my petite frame. But soon I'd be able to wear the student nurse uniform with its smart fitted blue checked-dress and belt with white starched collar, apron and hat. I stood anxiously waiting for Sister Kay, fully dressed in my sack, white starched hat, black stockings and flat, laced, sensible shoes. Sister Kay soon arrived: "Come along, Nurse Clark, I will take you to the ward where you will be working until you start your nurse training in April." She set off at speed down the corridor, with me close behind her. There was no going back now.

My teenage years were influenced by the sixties and free expression. Little did I know that nurse training was going to bring that to an end.

CHAPTER 38

Looking Back

Writing my childhood memoir has helped me to understand how much childhood and teenage years affect the rest of your life and shape you for the future. Upbringing, education, and social environment all play their part. Maybe I was destined to join the nursing profession.

The moments I remember from my early childhood are my most treasured, probably because I have carried them the longest. I wonder how accurate they all are. Maybe some details have been made up from looking at photographs and things I've been told. But surely a happy memory is worth hanging on to even if it isn't totally real. Memory is a tricky and unreliable thing, but those early recollections from my childhood appear to be the strongest and most vivid. I can still see so many memorable experiences: playing out in the fresh air, catching tadpoles in a stream, going to the beach, learning to ride my bike, buying penny sweets from the village shop, going to church and singing hymns, swimming lessons, school dinners, climbing trees and playing conkers, bonfire night, first day at secondary school, going out with friends without my parents, and my first crush – the list seems endless.

Following the tough and frugal times of the 1950s, the 1960s were a boom period, a time of changed attitudes and improved lifestyles. I have such fond memories of being a teenager in the Swinging Sixties. It was such a special time, full of fun, optimism and hope for the future. Dad continued to work hard, long hours and night shifts. In those days married men were deeply invested in the idea of being the male provider. Mum said that Dad was always "a good provider". I now listen to the classic hit of the sixties *A Hard Day's Night* by Lennon and McCartney in a different light. Lennon sings, "I work all day to get you money to buy you things." The lyrics were so relevant for the times.

I don't agree with the saying by Charles Fleischer "If you remember the sixties you really weren't there." I do remember the sixties and I was definitely there! It was the most interesting decade for me because of the huge changes that took place.

It was a glorious autumn day when I last visited Cullingworth hoping to capture memories from my youth. But I was bitterly disappointed to find that the area where I had grown up has been modernised, and the closing of many businesses and the mills has irrevocably altered the character of the local community. I can still identify with George's Square, incorporating St John's Church, the George pub and part of Station Road. It is the oldest part of the village and still retains a rural feel. But the nearby Francis Square has changed beyond recognition. The fruit shop where Marilynne grew up, like a lot of the old shops, has been converted into a dwelling. Rows of mill cottages, including Coronation street, occupied what is now the site of the old village hall. As I walk up Station Road, memories come flooding back. I pass the detached house where Dr Baird had his surgery, farmhouses, old terrace houses and the Conservative Club.

Houses have been built on the Four Fields where I spent so many happy times as a young child. I stop at my old primary school. It is no longer filled with the sound of children; it has been converted into flats. I can see myself on a cold winter's morning struggling to free myself from the sheets and blankets Mum had tucked me in so tightly, and rushing to get to the one heated room in the house, the kitchen, to get dressed for school. I remember how strict the school was and how we were punished for misbehaviour. Some of the kids didn't dare tell their parents if they'd been punished as they were likely to get walloped again! The village primary school moved from the original Victorian building to a new purpose-built site in 2004. It is a much bigger school taking around 270 pupils.

Mill Street and Lodge Street were demolished in the late sixties. I remember my mother being very upset having to leave the small terrace house they had worked so hard to buy. It took a long while for her to get over it. The area where the houses once stood looks so small and flat. How did so many houses fit into such a small space? I visualise running uphill to our house, the street full of life with women shouting to each other as they cleaned windows and scrubbed steps while delivery vans delivered their goods. A large Health Centre, newly opened Village Hall and Danchinos coffee shop now occupy the land where Lodge Street, Mill Street and the YMCA building once stood. An image of John O'Connor slumped in the ginnel suddenly springs to mind. The mill that once stood at the bottom of Mill Street has been converted into houses. I begin to feel quite sad walking along the main street to the rec where I spent so much of my childhood. It is unrecognisable; the large slide and swings, bowling green and tennis courts have all gone. Graffiti decorates the walls. I imagine Uncle Clifford waving to me from his garden.

A walk along the Great Northern Railway Trail lifts my spirits. The cycleway and footpath follow the route of a former railway, that of the Great Northern railway line between Bradford and Keighley that went via Queensbury and Cullingworth. The trail includes Cullingworth and Hewenden Viaduct. It is a pleasant walk through woodland out of the village, passing walkers, horse riders and people enjoying picnics while taking in the spectacular views. The railway trail is busy with young families out walking and riding their bicycles on the tarmacked surface. I wished it had been there when I was learning to ride my bike. Maybe I wouldn't have had as many bruises. The train was an important mode of transport when I was growing up and I must have travelled along this route many times, but have little memory of it. Leaving the trail I take the familiar route to Harecroft, turning into Bents Lane, where the scenery opens up to miles of breathtaking countryside with an array of vivid colours. I stopped to admire the majestic Hewenden Viaduct, the long bridge-like structure with its series of arches, standing in the autumn sunshine. I remember my friend Susan Ingham and me watching it carrying the railway across the valley. The sound of the train making its unique sounds as it chugged along with a trail of thick smoke behind it is a distant memory. I stop at the house where Susan lived and imagine her father looking out of the kitchen window waiting for her to arrive home from school. It was such a long walk for a young girl. It wouldn't be heard of these days, but they were different times. Goit Stock looked much the same, if a little overgrown, as I cross the bridge and head back to the village. I am amazed at how the village has grown, with many of the playing fields now replaced with large numbers of houses on the outskirts of the village. A stroll down Parkside Terrace brings back memories of my piano lessons with Mrs Cope. The houses were built in the 18th century for the mill workers and managers. They are just as I remember them. Parkside School, a coeducational secondary school, is now conveniently located in the area.

It is early afternoon when I arrive back in the village. I stop at the solid old mill buildings at Greenside Lane, surprised that they are now home to an international antiques centre. I can't resist having a look inside Antiques at the Mill. There is a real sense of history as I walk around the former worsted mill and memories of Mum come flooding back. It must have been a dreadful environment to work in. How was it possible to work long hours surrounded by noisy machinery, in the heated temperatures and contaminated atmosphere? I can picture the mill chimneys spewing out thick black smoke into the grimy air as I waited for Mum to finish work. She would leave the mill with a group of friends, all exhausted following a hard day's work. What would she think if she could see it today?

The village has now woken up with people rushing around, local shops doing good trade and the George busy with customers. It is more like the village I remember, but the place still feels quite soulless without my family. I find it difficult to imagine how hard their lives must have been before my birth. During the Great Depression, unemployment in 1930s' Britain was at crisis level with many living in abject poverty. Slum living and homelessness became common with their associated illnesses rife in certain parts of the country, particularly in the north of Scotland, where a sudden lack of demand for products meant sweeping unemployment. Unlike today, workers unemployment benefits were cut off after six months and the means test was introduced in 1931. If a family could not afford to pay the rent, their furniture and other assets would be seized. Grandma Field remembered food being in short supply, and women often going without so they could feed their families. The NHS was still a way off. Mum told me that if you were ill you had to go to a Panel doctor if you were eligible or see a doctor who would treat you for a fee. No wonder Dr Baird was well respected in the village. Six years of war and a subsequent age of austerity meant it would be a long time until the average Brit experienced prosperity again.

Sadly, I never knew my grandfathers. I was six years old when Grandad Field died and have no memories of him. Mum often spoke about him and I gather he was a quiet, gentle, kindly man who enjoyed spending time with me. Grandad Clark died in his fifties the year before my birth. Dad rarely spoke about him, but told me he never recovered from an accident in the Pit. I have learnt recently that following the Pit accident where there were fatalities, Grandad was hurt and so badly shocked his hair went grey overnight. Helen was a young girl when he died and remembers sitting on his knee and listening to him struggling to breathe. My grandfathers both suffered with respiratory problems. Was it the aftermath of working in the Pit? I think my grandads would have got along well together. I wish they'd have been around when I was growing up.

Writing my book has made me realise how little I know about my family. My life is like an unmade jigsaw puzzle, and

I am struggling to fit the pieces together. There are things about my family I will never know, because the people who did know are no longer here. There are so many questions I should have asked.

I had such a wonderful, carefree childhood, unaware of the economic hardship my parents were going through. But Mum and Dad enjoyed life and would remember the post-war era with great fondness. They often spoke about the good times we spent as a family. My parents had a long, happy marriage and continued to share many interests. They never lost their love of music and dancing. I remember them getting ready for the local tea dance, Dad looking very dapper in his flannel trousers, shirt and tie, and Mum wearing her posh dress and dancing shoes. It must have brought back memories of their youth. Dad became interested in opera while stationed in Italy during the war and I can still picture him, in later life, sitting quietly in his armchair listening to Luciano Pavarotti or Andrea Bocelli. Not a day goes by that I don't think about Mum and Dad. I will always miss them.

My parents were strict but fair and instilled a lot of values into me. They didn't display their emotions openly and I can't remember them telling me that they loved me. But they didn't need to. I was given the opportunities in life that they never had. It was because of their help and encouragement that I was able to pursue a successful career in the nursing profession. I feel such gratitude for what they did for me.

Postscript

As I put the final touches to this memoir the country is still in the grip of the Coronavirus pandemic.

I can't help but wonder what my parents would have made of the events of the last year. Doubtlessly, they would have been reminded of the war years, the hardship and difficulties, and the way everyone pulled together to get through the crisis.

I feel so proud of the heroic efforts of the NHS of which I was a part of for 46 years.

And the way in which scientists have worked at breakneck speed to develop vaccines against COVID-19 has been inspirational, giving us hope for the future.

Molly Brearley (nee Clark)
Silsden, West Yorkshire.
Date 10th February 2021

Also by the Same Author

Molly Brearley's memoir begins in the mid-1960's, as a naïve seventeen year old, leaving the security of her family home to start nurse training in Huddersfield.

Friendships soon develop with other young nurses as they struggle to cope with strict discipline, late-night studying and long working hours.

It is a decade of major change, the disaster of the war over we are experiencing more freedom, enabling us to enjoy the little free time we have. Being a group of mischievous teenagers, we soon start to break the rules, sneaking out of the nurses' home at every opportunity for a night at the disco. What an impossible job the home sister had trying to keep us all in order.

Many changes were also happening in the NHS. Nurses were full of optimism; they started to feel more confident and were beginning to develop greater independence. Career opportunities were greater than they had previously been. It was a fascinating time to be a teenager working in the nursing profession.

AVAILABLE FROM WWW.YPDBOOKS.COM

ISBN: 978-0-9954759-0-8

Molly was unsure what she wanted to do next. Having worked as a General nurse and Midwife, she was now ready for a new challenge.

In 1979 she found herself attending an interview for the Health Visiting course not having a clue what she was letting herself in for.

This sequel to *The Calling: Life as student nurse in the 1960s*, follows the authors experiences as she is drawn into the world of Health Visiting. The job soon proved to be more challenging than expected as she re-calls the pressure she had to contend with as a newly qualified Health Visitor. What followed was a career in Health Visiting spanning over thirty-two years working in the Keighley and Burley-in-Wharfedale areas of West Yorkshire.
The book is written with understanding, humour and candour as she shares real stories about real people. Some stories are heart-breaking but there are lots of light-hearted moments with many laughs along the way. It also gives a glimpse into the changes in health visiting practice over the years.

AVAILABLE FROM WWW.YPDBOOKS.COM

ISBN: 978-0-9954759-1-5